MW01286035

Financial Terms Dictionary

Investment Terminology Explained

Published June 30, 2017

Revision 1.1

Financial Terms Dictionary

Copyright And Trademark Notices

Limits of Liability and Disclaimer of Warranties

The materials in this book are provided "as is" and without warranties of any kind either express or implied. The Author disclaims all warranties, express or implied, including, but not limited to, implied warranties of merchantability and fitness for a particular purpose.

The Author does not warrant that defects will be corrected, or that that the site or the server that makes this eBook available are free of viruses or other harmful components. The Author does not warrant or make any representations regarding the use or the results of the use of the materials in this book in terms of their correctness, accuracy, reliability, or otherwise. Applicable law may not allow the exclusion of implied warranties, so the above exclusion may not apply to you.

Under no circumstances, including, but not limited to, negligence, shall the Author be liable for any special or consequential damages that result from the use of, or the inability to use this eBook, even if the Author or his authorised representative has been advised of the possibility of such damages.

Applicable law may not allow the limitation or exclusion of liability or incidental or consequential damages, so the above limitation or exclusion may not apply to you. In no event shall the Author's total liability to you for all damages, losses, and causes of action (whether in contract, tort, including but not limited to, negligence or otherwise) exceed the amount paid by you, if any, for this eBook.

Facts and information are believed to be accurate at the time they were placed in this book. All data provided in this book is to be used for information purposes only. The information contained within is not intended to provide specific legal, financial or tax advice, or any other advice whatsoever, for any individual or company and should not be relied upon in that regard. The services described are only offered in jurisdictions where they may be legally offered. Information provided is not all-inclusive, and is limited to information that is made available and such information should not be relied upon as all-inclusive or accurate.

You are advised to do your own due diligence when it comes to making business decisions and should use caution and seek the advice of qualified professionals. You should check with your accountant, lawyer, or professional advisor, before acting on this or any information. You may not consider any examples, documents, or other content in this eBook or otherwise provided by the Author to be the equivalent of professional advice.

The Author assumes no responsibility for any losses or damages resulting from your use of any link, information, or opportunity contained in this book or within any other information disclosed by the author in any form whatsoever.

About the Author

Thomas Herold is a successful entrepreneur and personal development coach. After a career with one of the largest electronic companies in the world, he realised that a regular job would never fully satisfy his need for connection on a deep level. The only way to live his full potential was to start building his own business and find new ways to be in service to others.

For over 25 years he has helped many people - including himself - build their dream businesses. Toward that goal, he focuses on education, simplified and enhanced by modern technology. He is the author of 15 books with over 200,000 copies distributed worldwide.

Other than his passion for creating businesses, Thomas has spent over 20 years in the self-development field. Placing emphasis on the exploration of consciousness and building practical applications that allow people to express their purpose and passion in life, Thomas's work in this area has provided ample and happy proof that this approach works.

He believes that every person has at least one gift and that, when this gift is developed and nourished, it will serve as a fountainhead of personal happiness and help contribute to a better, more sustainable world.

For the past twelve years Thomas has studied the monetary system and has experienced some profound insights on how money and wealth are related. He has recently committed to sharing this financial knowledge in a new venture - the Financial Terms Dictionary, a hub of financial term descriptions designed to help people get started on their own money makeover and get a financial education in the process.

Thomas's ultimate vision for the Financial Terms Dictionary is to empower people to adopt a wealthy mindset and to create abundance for themselves and others. His ability to explain complex information in simple terms makes him an outstanding teacher and coach.

For more information please visit: Financial Terms Dictionary

Financial Dictionary Series

There are 12 books in this financial dictionaries series available. Click the links below to see an overview and available formats. There is also a premium edition available, which covers over 900 financial terms!

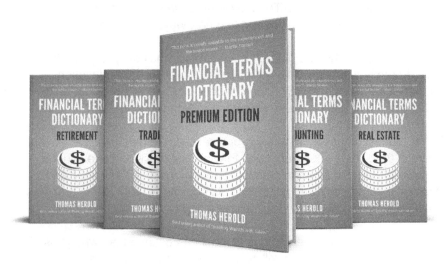

Standard Editions
Financial Terms Dictionary - Accounting Edition
Financial Terms Dictionary - Banking Edition
Financial Terms Dictionary - Corporate Finance Edition
Financial Terms Dictionary - Economics Edition
Financial Terms Dictionary - Investment Edition
Financial Terms Dictionary - Laws & Regulations Edition
Financial Terms Dictionary - Real Estate Edition
Financial Terms Dictionary - Retirement Edition
Financial Terms Dictionary - Trading Edition
Financial Terms Dictionary - Acronyms Edition

Basic & Premium Editions
Financial Terms Dictionary - Basic Edition
Financial Terms Dictionary - Premium Edition

Table Of Contents

401(k) Plan

401k retirement plans are specific kinds of accounts that the government established to help individuals to plan and save for retirement. Individuals fund these accounts using pre-taxed dollars from payrolls.

People invest money in these accounts into several different types of investments. These include stocks, mutual funds, and bonds. Gains earned in the account include dividends, capital gains, and interest. These gains do not get taxed until the owners withdraw the funds.

The name of the 401k comes from the portion of Internal Revenue Service Code which pertains to it. This vehicle for saving for retirement began in 1981 when an act of Congress created it.

There are a number of benefits to 401k accounts that recommend them to individuals. Five of these include tax benefits, flexibility of investments, employer matching programs, loan abilities, and portability.

The advantageous tax benefits are one of the main reasons that 401k plans are so popular. Money contributed does not become taxable until individuals withdraw it. Similarly gains accrued in the account are also tax-deferred. Over several decades, this makes a significant difference in the amount of money that people can save.

Investments that the IRS allows in these 401k retirement plans provide some flexibility. Those who do not want to take on much risk can choose to put more of their funds into shorter term bonds which are lower risk. Others who are more concerned with developing wealth over the long term can put a larger percentage of the money into equities like stocks and mutual funds. Company stock can also be acquired at a discount with many employers.

A tremendous edge that these 401k retirement plans provide their owners is the employer match feature. A great number of employers match their employees' contributions as a company benefit. This is done on a percentage basis. Newer employees may receive a 25% of contributions match, while employees who have been at a company longer may receive 50% or even 100% matches. Matches are only made on a certain maximum percentage of income that an employee contributes. This is the closest thing to free money a person can obtain at work.

Loan abilities from 401k retirements are a helpful feature for individuals in times of need. When people find themselves needing money with no other place to turn, the government permits them to obtain 401k loans from the plan. The plan administrator has to approve it as well. Loans from 401k plans are not taxed or penalized so long as they are repaid according to the repayment schedule and terms.

There are no restrictions on the uses of such loans. Some employers have minimum amounts that can be borrowed of $1,000 and a maximum number of loans an employee can take at a time. Sometimes employees will have to get their spouse's written consent before the company will issue the loan.

There are limits on the amount of a balance that can be borrowed. This is typically as much as 50% of the vested balance to no more than $50,000. When an employer will not allow an employee to take out a loan against the plan, hardship withdrawals can be requested. These are taxed and also penalized at a 10% rate.

Portability means the 401k retirement plan can go with the employees as they change jobs. Investors have four different choices for their 401k plan when they move to another company. They can choose to leave the plan with the old employer and pay any administration fees for the account staying there. They might instead do a rollover of their account to the new employer's 401k retirement plan.

A third option is to convert the 401k retirement plan into an Individual Retirement Account. Finally they might decide to close the 401k and receive the proceeds in cash. This would mean all money would be subject to taxes and the 10% penalty fee.

403(b) Plan

403(b) plans were created for employees of schools, churches, and tax exempt organizations. Individuals who are eligible may establish and maintain their own 403(b) accounts. Their employers can and often do make contributions to the employees' accounts. Individuals are able to open one of three different types of 403(b)s.

The first is an annuity plan that an insurance company establishes. These types of plans are sometimes called TDAs tax deferred annuities or TSAs tax sheltered annuities. A second plan type is an account which a retirement custodian offers and manages. With these 403(b)s, the account holders may only choose from mutual funds and regulated investment companies that the custodian allows. The final type is a retirement income account. These accounts accept a combination of mutual funds or annuities for the investment choices.

Employers have some control over these accounts. They are able to decide which financial institution will hold the employees' 403(b) accounts. This determines the kind of plan that the employees are able to set up and fund. Employers receive several advantages from choosing to offer a 403(b).

The benefits which they get to offer their employees are worthwhile. This helps to ensure valuable employees stay with the organization. They also enjoy sharing the funding costs between themselves and their employees. Employers may also choose for the 403(b) to only accept employee contributions if they do not wish to participate financially in the account.

Employees also experience several benefits from these types of retirement vehicles. They may contribute tax deferred dollars from their income. They may also contribute taxed dollars to the accounts. In these Roth 403(b)s, all of their earnings accrue tax free for the entire life of the account. Deferred tax payments until retirement typically allow for the employees to pay fewer taxes as they are often in a more advantageous tax bracket at retirement point. Employees may also obtain loans from their 403(b) accounts as they need them.

A variety of non profit organizations may choose to establish such a 403(b) plan for their employees. This includes any 501(c)(3) tax exempt organization, co-op hospital service organizations, public school systems, ministers at churches, Native American public school systems, and (USUHS) Uniformed Services for the University of the Health Sciences.

Such 403(b) plans can obtain a variety of contribution types. Employees may have elective deferral contributions taken out of each paycheck. These are taken out in a pretax dollars arrangement. Employees also have the ability to contribute taxed dollars to the accounts. They have these deducted from their payrolls as well.

Employers may also choose to make contributions which are either discretionary or fixed amounts as they desire. Employees and employers may make contributions to Roth 403(b) accounts. These 403(b) accounts may also receive any combination of the previously mentioned contribution types, which demonstrates their flexibility.

Employees have generous annual contribution limits with these plans. In 2016, they may contribute up to $18,000 (or $24,000 if they are over 50 years old and catching up on contributions for retirement). For 2016, employers may also deposit as much as $53,000 (up to 100% of the employee compensation) as an annual contribution.

Regarding distributions, the rules are comparable to the other types of retirement savings vehicles. Distributions of deferred taxed dollars become taxable like regular income when the employee receives them. If these are taken before the employee turns 59 ½, then the withdrawn dollars are assessed the standard 10% penalty for early withdrawals. There are some exceptions to this penalty for which an employee may qualify. One of these exceptions is if the employee terminates the job even before reaching the age of retirement.

408(k) Plan

The 408(k) Plan is a retirement plan that employers set up to assist their employees in saving money for their post working years. It is named for the section of the IRS code that describes these accounts. Though there are some distinctions, a 408(k) Plan is actually a simpler version of the ever popular 401(k) plan.

These 408(k)'s are intended for smaller companies which employ fewer than 25 staff. Self employed individuals are also able to take advantage of these plans. SEP Simplified Employee Pensions are another name for the 408(k)'s.

These plans are practical and useful for workers because they are able to contribute dollars that have not yet been taxed. In addition to helping them save for retirement, it lowers their net incomes for the tax year in question. This can reduce the tax bracket into which the employees fall. It leads to lower taxes for the individuals who contribute. The deposits do not become taxable as income until the point where the employees take their money back in the form of distributions.

Employers are also able to contribute funds to the account on behalf of the employees and in their names. The employer contributions are similarly tax deductible. Besides providing the employer with a nice benefit to offer their workers, it saves them on their annual company tax bill as well. Though these accounts are set up by employers, they remain in the name of the employees and for their sole benefits.

408(k) plans share many features with their 401(k) cousins. The 408(k)'s are somewhat simpler to understand, set up, and utilize. Both plans have yearly maximum contribution limits. With these plans, the employees also do not pay any taxes for contributions which the employer makes in the account. Both accounts are also tax deferred.

Taxes will only become due when the employee takes distributions at the retirement age starting at 59 and a half. Until that point, none of the money they contribute will be treated like income. There are some limitations and restrictions on these kinds of accounts. They can be utilized by self employed individuals and smaller companies. They may not be set up by larger companies which count more than 25 employees.

Employees can not contribute more than the maximum annual limit to these accounts. If they do, the surplus dollars will be treated as income, taxed, and also penalized by 10%. Money which an employee takes out early before retirement age is also subject to taxes and 10% penalties.

There is an exception to this early withdrawal rule. If an employee feels the financial need, he or she is allowed to take money back without penalties on a loan basis only. 408(k) plans do allow for such loans, provided that they are repaid. The money must be paid back to the account according to a payment schedule set up with the plan administrator. In the even that it is not put back, the loan amount becomes treated as an early withdrawal distribution. In this case, the full tax and 10% penalty amount will apply to the total loan principle.

The maximum contribution amounts to the 408(k) Plans vary by year. The IRS increases the limits from time to time to compensate for projected inflation. When employees reach 50, they are allowed to increase their contributions per year to an IRS allowed larger dollar amount. This is to help them to catch up on any contributions which they may have missed out on over the years.

412(i) Plan

412(i) Plans are pension plans that are classified as qualified defined benefit arrangements. They were established by the IRS for small companies and self employed business owners to have a way to save for their retirement and those of their employees. Employers fund these plans with only fixed annuities or both annuities and permanent life insurance.

For the 412(i) Plans to be qualified and legal, they must meet the standards for these kinds of plans. This includes non discrimination rules and eligibility requirements. All employees of the firm who are over 20 years old must be included if they have worked there for at least a year.

These plans have become more popular with time. This is in part because employers fund them with guaranteed investments. When they contribute fixed annuities, the retirement benefits are figured by utilizing the annuity's guaranteed purchase rate. If life insurance contracts are contributed, benefits are based on the guaranteed cash accumulation of the policies. One advantage this gives the small business owner is the ability to fund contributions in dollar amounts which are larger than the amounts that competing qualified plans allow. The contributions they make are also tax deductible. This reduces the tax burden for the contribution year.

There are several benefits that these plans feature. The monthly benefit for the account holder is guaranteed. They create large income tax deductions for the benefits of the employers. Besides this these plans offer significant death benefits for the account holders. These mean that these 412(i) Plans provide small businesses with an attractive package for obtaining and keeping important talent. They also help the small company's employees who can count on the guaranteed and fixed benefits at retirement.

412(i) Plans are special because they do not have to live up to complicated rules for funding them adequately. There are also no yearly actuarial requirements to certify that the plan is properly funded. The guaranteed parts of the fixed annuities and life insurance vehicles ensure that these defined benefit plans will be solvent. The only requirement to ensure that this happens is for the employer to continuously pay the annual policy or annuity premiums.

The life insurance company provides all of the guarantees that the plan requires. One important feature of these and other defined benefit plans is that they do not always allow account holders to take loans out of the plan. The Pension Protection Act of 2006 set out many of the standards for these plans and also provided an alternative number of 412(e)(3) for them.

If annuity policies yield a greater amount of dividends or interest than is guaranteed, this benefits the employer. The plan rules stipulate that the extra payments credit against upcoming premiums. If the life insurance contract offers dividends, these are also applied against premiums in the future. They do not go to the account holder, but always to reduce the premiums of the 412(i) Plans.

There are important reasons that employers choose to include a contract of life insurance in such 412(i) Plans. They offer fully tax deductible ways of giving the small business owner and employees death benefits. When the beneficiary receives this benefit, the face value minus the cash value (of the policy's death benefit) distributes as a tax free income. This life insurance contained within the plan gives the account holders valuable estate liquidity that it will likely need after they have passed away.

The insurance companies which offer the annuity contract or the insurance policy for the plan do not usually provide administration for the 412(i) Plans. This service is typically supplied by IRS approved third party administrators.

457(b) Plan

A 457(b) plan is a retirement savings vehicle. It derives its name from the Internal Revenue Service code that regulates the plans in its section 457(b). Many times this retirement account name is simply shortened to 457 Plan.

There are many similarities between these 457 Plans and tax deferred, employer provided retirement vehicles including 403(b) and 401(k) plans. All of these retirement vehicles are defined contribution plans. People who participate in these 457 Plans set up payroll deductions so that a portion of their income is put into this investment account that is tax free.

The government established these 457 Plans in 1978. They were set up to be another defined contribution account that would help two particular kinds of employers. They are intended for both government employers and non government employers which are tax exempt as with hospitals and charities.

Despite this fact, a few different rules apply for the government plans as opposed to the non government plans. The principle difference revolves around funding. Government 457 Plans have to be funded by the employer in question. The non government 457 Plans are practically all funded by employees. The vast majority of 457(b) plans that private not for profit companies use they only offer to well paid employees usually in upper level management.

With 457 Plans, there must be both a plan administrator and a plan provider. Each plan provides its own limited choices for investment options which are particular to the plan.

Rollover rules are different for these 457 Plans as well. The non government versions can not be transferred over to qualified retirement plans which include IRA and 401(k)s. Instead they can only be rolled over to other tax exempt 457 Plans. The rules are different with government sponsored employer plans. These may be transferred into another employer's 401(k), 403(b), or 457(b) plan as well as to an IRA account. The new plan must permit account holders to make such transfers.

Withdrawals are easier for government sponsored plans as well. Individuals may do early withdrawals before they reach the 59 ½ year old age of retirement and not have to suffer the 10% early withdrawal penalty. The full withdrawn amount would be taxed as regular income. Employees who are switching jobs may also keep the money where it is assuming the plan permits this.

Rollover rules on 457(b) plans are pretty standard. If funds are dispersed to the account owner, he or she has a maximum of 60 days to finish the rollover process. Beyond this time, the IRS considers this money to have been distributed and to be taxable. Owners are also restricted to doing a single rollover in a calendar year with these retirement vehicles.

The date on which the owners receive their 457 Plan distribution is when the one year rule commences. While the money is in the 60 day process of being rolled over, it may not be invested. Direct rollovers avoid the dangers of the 60 day rule. An account holder never obtains a distribution check (as with indirect rollovers) in this type of transfer. Instead, the plan provider will directly transfer all money to the new IRA or retirement plan.

Investment choices in 457 Plans are more limited than with Self Directed IRAs or Solo 401(k) plans. The plan provider will restrict choices to ones that fit their plan. If they permit them, owners may invest their funds in individual bonds and stocks, fixed or indexed annuities, exchange traded funds, and mutual funds.

Gold bullion can not be purchased by these plans. Paper gold investments such as stocks of gold mining firms, mutual funds containing gold mining companies, or gold ETFs like GLD and mining ETFs may be purchased instead.

AAA Rating

AAA Rating refers to the maximum potential credit rating that a credit ratings bureau can award to an issuing entity's bonds. Such a credit rating represents a superb level of creditworthiness. It means that the issuing entity is easily capable of meeting its various financial obligations. The three major ratings agencies of Moody's, Standard & Poor's, and Fitch Ratings all utilize the AAA as their top credit rating which designates those bonds and issuers which have the highest possible level of credit quality.

It is not possible to completely eliminate the potential risk of a credit default from a bond issuer. Yet those entities which possess AAA rated bonds are believed to have the least possible chance of defaulting on their interest payments or principal repayments. Because of this, such bonds provide their investors with the smallest possible yields of any bonds that possess the same dates of maturity.

Thanks to the Global Financial Crisis of 2008, many companies and countries lost their coveted AAA rating. In fact, by the middle of 2009, there were only four remaining firms out of the entire list of S&P 500 companies that still held their treasured AAA rated credit. The story was the same with the gold standard credit rated nations of the world as well.

Before the Great Recession, a number of nations enjoyed the highly coveted AAA credit rating from all three of the big three ratings agencies. Once the dust had settled, only the following nine nations still held it including Australia, Canada, Denmark, Germany, Luxembourg, Norway, Singapore, Sweden, and Switzerland. Countries that had lost it included Austria, Finland, France, the United Kingdom, and the United States. The U.S. still had the AAA rated credit from Moody's and Fitch, while the United Kingdom still held it from Standard & Poor's (who even removed it from negative watch).

High credit ratings like the AAA rating provide significant benefits to a company or nation which carries them. It allows the issuer to borrow at a reduced interest rate and ultimate cost. These companies and countries are also able to borrow greater amounts of money when they possess the highest ratings. Lower costs of borrowing allow for nations and corporations to access opportunities through cheap and easy credit. A company might be able to buy out a competitor as it is able to cheaply borrow the money for the transaction costs of the relevant merger and acquisition.

Where companies are concerned, it is possible for them to enjoy the highest AAA rating on bonds which they issue as secured while having a lower credit rating on those which are unsecured. This is simply because secured bonds provide a particular asset that has been put up as collateral in case the issuer defaults on the interest or principal payments of the bond in question. The creditor has the right to seize the asset if the issuer ends up defaulting. Such bonds could carry the collateral of real estate, machinery, or other forms of equipment. Conversely, unsecured bonds only carry the backing of the issuer's capability of repaying the obligation. This is why the credit ratings for unsecured forms of bonds only rely on the income source of the issuer in question.

Since the Global Financial Crisis destroyed the highest creditworthiness of many a long-standing AAA rated nation, neither the world's largest debtor nor creditor nations possess the all-important AAA rating. For example, S&P argues that it will only deliver the AAA rating in the cases where an "extremely strong capacity to meet financial commitments" exists.

The euro zone was long a shining example of many nations which possessed unanimous AAA rated credit. After the Great Recession and Sovereign Debt Crisis ravaged Europe, only the two nations of Luxembourg and Germany still retain this three ratings agency unanimous AAA status.

Agency Bonds

Agency bonds are those bonds that are actually issued by United States' government sponsored entities. This means that these bonds are not government guaranteed, as they are created by private companies. They are backed up implicitly by the United States government, since these organizations were created to permit some categories of individuals to have the ability to receive lower cost financing, in particular first time home buyers and students.

The biggest, best recognized names in Agency Bond issuers prove to be Sallie Mae, Freddie Mac, and Fannie Mae. These three large companies are different from government agencies in that they are not guaranteed by the United States' government's promise of full faith and credit. Instead, they are all privately held and run companies that are given government charters as a result of their critical activities that carry out government directed policies.

Agency bonds are used to raise money to help these companies offer farm loans, home loans, student loans, and international trade financing. As a result of the government deeming these activities to be significant enough to grant charters, the markets consider that the Federal Government will not permit these chartered firms to go under. This gives their agency bonds the implied government sponsored entity guarantee. As a result of this implicit guarantee, these agency bonds carry ratings and yields that are comparable to government issued debt.

As an example, Private Export Funding Corporation bonds prove to be backed up by actual collateral of United States government securities. Federal Farm Credit Banks' bonds are not, although it is a government sponsored entity. Despite the differences, the yield-to-maturity of the two bonds are 4.753% and 4.760% respectively. These two organizations' debt obligations are nearly priced the same, demonstrating once again the implicit guarantee in the government sponsored entity securities.

The issue of taxation is another important one to consider when you are looking at Agency Bonds. All agency bonds are taxable on Federal levels. Many are not taxed on state levels. This is critical if you are an investor who resides in a state that has its own taxes. The interest payments from the best known of these organizations like Freddie Mac and Fannie Mae can be taxed on a state level. The majority of others agency bonds avoid this taxation, making their rates more attractive for many investors.

The vast majority of all agency bonds outstanding, more than ninety percent, are issued by only the four largest government sponsored entities. By largest size, these are Federal Home Loan Banks, Federal Home Loan Mortgage Corporation, Federal National Mortgage Association, and Federal Farm Credit Banks. The Federal Home Loan Banks' and Federal Farm Credit Banks' agency bonds are not state income taxable.

Amortization

The word amortization is one that is commonly utilized by financial officers of corporations and accountants. They utilize it when they are working with time concepts and how they relate to financial statements of accounts. You typically hear this word employed when you are figuring up loan calculations, or when you are determining interest payments.

The concept of amortization possesses a lengthy history and it is currently employed in numerous different segments of finance. The word itself descends from Middle English. Here amortisen meant to "alienate" or "kill" something. This derivation itself comes from the Latin admortire that signified "plus death." It is loosely related to the derivation of the word mortgage, as well.

This accounting principle is much like depreciation that diminishes a liability or asset's value over a given period of time through payments. It covers the practical life span of a tangible asset. With liabilities, it includes a pre-set amount of time over which money is paid back. Like this, a certain amount of money is set aside for the loan repayment over its lifetime.

Even though depreciation is similar to amortization, they are not the same concepts. The main difference between them lies in what they cover. While depreciation is most commonly employed to describe physical assets like property, vehicles, or buildings, amortization instead covers intangibles such as product development, copyrights, or patents. Where liabilities are concerned, it relates to income in the future that will be paid out over a given amount of time. Depreciation is instead a lost income over a time period.

Several different kinds of amortization are presently in use. This varies with the accounting method that is practiced. Business amortization deals with borrowed funds and loans and the paying of particular amounts in different time frames. When used as amortization analysis, this is the means of cost execution analysis for a given group of operations. Where tax law is concerned, amortization pertains to the interest amount that is paid over a given span of time relevant to payments and tax rates.

Amortization can also be employed with regards to zoning rules and regulations, since it conveys a property owner's time for relocating as a result of zoning guidelines and pre-existing use. Another variation is used as negative amortization. This pertains specifically to increasing loan amounts that result from total interest due not being paid up at the appropriate time.

Amortization can also be employed over a widely ranging time frame. It could cover only a year or extend to as many as forty years. This depends on the kind of loan or asset utilized. Some examples include building loans that span over as many as forty years and car loans that commonly span over merely four to five years. Asset examples would be patent right expenses that commonly are spread out over seventeen years.

Annual Percentage Yield (APY)

APY describes the amount of compound interest which individuals or businesses will earn in a given year (or longer time period). Investments in money market accounts, savings accounts, and CD Certificates of Deposit all pay out such interest. It is the annual percentage yield that demonstrates precisely the amount in interest individuals will receive. This is helpful for people or businesses trying to ascertain which investments and banks offer superior returns by comparing and contrasting their real yields. In general, higher Annual Percentage Yields are better to have (unless one is comparing interest on credit card debts).

This APY is practical to understand and measure simply because it considers compound interest and the miracle of compounding within any account. Simple interest rates do not do this. Compounding is simply earning interest on interest that has already accrued and been paid. It signifies that individuals are gaining a greater amount in interest than the corresponding interest rate literally indicates.

It is always a good idea to consider a real world example for clarification purposes. If Fred deposits $10,000 into a particular savings account that provides a two percent yearly interest rate, then at the end of that first year Fred will have $10,200. This assumes that the interest is paid one time per year. If the bank were to figure up and pay out the interest on a daily basis, it would increase the amount to $10,202. The extra $2 may seem small, but given a longer time frame of from 10 to 30 years, this amount can add up, particularly if larger deposits are involved.

APY should never be confused with APR. They have some similarities, but APR does not consider compounding. It is once again a simpler means of computing interest. Credit card loans are an area where it is important to understand the differences between annual percentage rate and annual percentage yield. When people carry a balance, they will be paying higher APY's then the APR the firm actually quotes. This is because interest is assessed monthly, which means that interest on the interest will be computed on each following month.

The key to obtaining a better APY on investments and savings accounts lies in getting as frequent a compounding period as possible. Quarterly compounding is better than annually, yet daily is the most superior form of compounding possible. This means that as individuals are looking to increase their APY's personally, it is important to have the money compounding as frequently as they can practically achieve.

When two CD Certificates of Deposit pay out the same rate, it is best to select that one which actually pays out both more frequently and also boasts the greater APY. With CD's, the interest payments become automatically reinvested. More frequent reinvestment is always better. This will help any individual or business to earn a greater amount of interest on the interest payments already earned and paid out.

Calculating the annual percentage yield is not an easy task. Business calculators as well as computer algorithms mostly do it for people nowadays. The simplest way to find the APY for a given account is to plug in the information including the initial deposit, compounding frequency period, interest rate, and amount of overall time for the period considered. These smart calculators will then tell you both the effective annual percentage yield as well as the ending balance on the hypothetical account at the end of the given time period.

Arbitrage

Arbitrage refers to the practice of taking advantage of the price imbalances sometimes arising in two or even more markets. People who work in foreign money exchange run their whole businesses on this model. As an example, they look for tourists who require a rapid exchange of their cash for the local currency. Tourists agree to accept this local money for a lower amount than the actual market rate, and the money changer gets to keep the spread created by the higher rate that he charges them for the local currency. This spread that the different rates create becomes his profit.

Many different scenarios allow for investors or businessmen to become involved in the arbitrage practice. Sometimes, one market is not aware of the existence of the second market, or it simply can not access it. Arbitrageurs, persons who avail themselves of arbitrage, are also able to benefit from the different liquidities present in various markets.

Arbitrage is typically employed to discuss opportunities with investments and money rather than price imbalances for goods. Because of arbitrageurs operating in various markets whenever they spot opportunities, the prices found in the higher market will commonly drop while the prices in the lower market will usually rise so that they meet somewhere around the middle of the price difference. The phrase efficiency of the market then deals with the rate of speed at which these differing prices converge towards each other.

There are people who make arbitrage their livelihood. Working in arbitrage offers the possibilities of lucrative gains and profits. It does not come free of risk though. The greatest danger is that the prices may change rapidly between the varying markets. As an example, the spreads could rapidly fluctuate in only the tiny amount of time that is necessary for the two transactions to take place. In instances where these prices are moving quickly, arbitrageurs may not only find that they missed the chance to realize the profit between the differences in the prices, but that in fact they lost money on the deal.

Examples of arbitrage in the financial markets abound. Convertible arbitrage is working with convertible bonds to realize arbitrage. The bond can be converted into stock of the issuer of the bond. Sometimes, the amounts of shares that the bond will convert to are worth more than the price of the bond. In this case, an arbitrageur will be able to make a profit by purchasing the bond, converting it into the stock shares, and then selling the stock on the exchange to realize the difference.

Relative value arbitrage is using options to acquire the underlying shares of stock. It might be that the option is less expensive relative to the shares of stock that it will purchase. If a stock trades at $200, and the option that permits you to buy a share of the stock for $120 is trading at only $50, then you could buy the option, exercise it for the shares, and sell it for $200. You would only have spent $170 per share on the purchase, and then realize a $30 per share profit.

Asset Allocation

Asset allocation involves diversifying an investor portfolio into a variety of different assets based on the appropriate level of risk. This procedure has investors divide up their investments between varying types of assets. Among these might be stocks, real estate, bonds, and cash.

The goal is to maximize the reward and risk balance using the investors' own goals and scenarios. This has become one of the critical ideas behind money management and financial planning today. There are several different types of asset allocation to consider. These are strategic, tactical, and dynamic.

In strategic asset allocation, the investor sets out target allocations for the desired different classes of assets. When the percentage balance deviates from the original set levels, it will involve the investor rebalancing the overall portfolio. The allocations will be reset to the original ones as they change significantly because of different returns that each class earns.

Strategic asset allocation sets these initial allocations up using a number of different considerations. Among these are the investor objectives, the intended time frame of investing, and the risk tolerance. These allocations can be changed in time as the different variables alter.

A good comparison to this form of allocating is a traditional buy and hold investment strategy. This form of strategic allocating of assets and the tactical allocation approach are both derived from modern portfolio theory. They seek diversification so that they can lower risk and boost the returns on portfolios.

Tactical asset allocating is more active than strategic forms of the discipline. Investors who follow tactical allocating will re-balance the asset percentages in different categories on a more regular basis. They will do this in an effort to benefit from market sectors that are stronger or poised for gains. They might also re-balance in an effort to capture anomalies in market pricing.

Tactical allocating is well suited to professional portfolio managers. They study the markets and look to find extra returns from scenarios that develop. This is still only considered to be a strategy that is moderately active. When the short term gains are attained, these managers go back to the original strategic asset balance of the portfolio.

Investors or managers who look for tactical asset allocators often choose ETF exchange traded funds or index funds for this purpose. The goal of these vehicles concentrates on asset classes rather than individual investments. This reduces the costs of rebalancing. The transaction costs of buying and selling index funds is far less than with many individual stocks or even several mutual funds.

For an individual investor, they allow them to pick a stock index fund, bond index fund, and money market fund. It is also possible to focus on sub-sectors within the bigger funds. There are foreign stocks, large cap stocks, individual sectors, and small cap stock funds or ETFs from which to choose.

When tactical allocating in sectors, investors can pick out those which they believe will perform strongly for either the near term or intermediate time frames. Those that believe health and technology will do well in upcoming months or even a few years might rebalance some of the portfolio into ETFs in those industry segments.

With dynamic asset allocation, investors are focused on re-balancing the portfolio to keep it near its long term goals of asset mix. This means that positions in assets classes that are outperforming have to be reduced. Those that are under-performing must then be increased with the proceeds from the outperforming assets. This restores the portfolio mix to the desired allocation. The reason investors would do this is to keep the original asset mix so that they can capture appropriate returns that meet or beat the target benchmark.

Asset Backed Security (ABS)

An Asset Backed Security is also known by its acronym ABS. This refers to a type of financial security. These are commonly backed up using either a lease, a loan, or receivables against company assets (which would not include either mortgage backed securities or real estate). With the world of investing, such ABS provide other choices for those who wish to invest in something other than common corporate debt issues.

It is interesting to note that these Asset Backed Securities are more or less identical to MBS Mortgage Backed Securities. The primary difference lies in the securities which back the two financial instruments. With the ABS, they can include credit card debt, leases, loans, royalties, and even the receivables of the company issuing the debt. Yet these mortgage based securities may never underlie the ABS.

Such an Asset Backed Security delivers to the issuer of the security a means of creating more cash for the business. It allows yield hungry investors the chance to sink their money into a great range of assets which generate income. It is worth noting that most of these underlying assets will not be liquid. This means that they can not be readily sold as stand alone assets. Yet in pooling such assets into a single conglomeration, a financial security may be created. This is done in the process referred to as securitization. This permits the asset owner to employ them in a marketable fashion.

Among the assets of such pools could be car loans, home equity loans, student loans, credit card receivables, or other anticipated cash flow items. The capacity of Asset Backed Security issuers to be creative should never be underestimated. There have even been ABS which were established utilizing the cash flow generated by movie release revenues, aircraft leases, creative works and other forms of royalty payments, and even solar energy photovoltaic revenue streams. Practically any scenario where cash is produced can be packaged up via securitization into an ABS.

It is often helpful to consider an example of this somewhat complicated Asset Backed Security topic. Consider the case of a fictitious firm Car Loans For Everybody. When individuals wish to borrow funds to purchase a car, Car Loans For Everybody will issue them the cash in a check. The individual will have to pay back the loan along with a specified interest amount at a certain time in monthly installments. It could be that Car Loans is so successful at making automobile loans that they deplete their cash reserves and can no longer issue additional loans. They have the ability to sell off their present book of loans to the fictitious investment firm Imperial Legends. Imperial Legends will then provide them with the cash they need to continue issuing new loans.

This is only where the securitization process begins. Imperial Legends investment firm would then arrange the bought out loans into a collection of parcels known in the business as tranches. A tranche effectively is a batch of loans that posses similar features. This would include interest rates, maturity dates, and anticipated rates of delinquency. After this, the Imperial Legends firm would offer new securities with features much like bonds in every tranche they created.

Finally, investors will buy such securities. They obtain the underlying cash flow out of the pool of car loans, less the administration fee, which Imperial Legends will keep to cover their costs and towards their profit.

There are three typical types of tranches in an Asset Backed Security. These are commonly referred to as Class A, Class B, and Class C. Senior most tranches belong to Class A. They are generally the biggest tranche. They will be structured in such a way as to obtain a decent investment rating so that they are easily marketable to investors.

With the Class B tranche, the credit quality will necessarily be lower. This inversely means that the yield will be higher than that of the senior tranche. Since the risk is greater, investors need to be compensated for their appropriate risk of defaults.

Class C tranche has the lowest credit rating of all. It could be the credit quality is so poor that investors will refuse to consider it altogether. In such cases, the ABS issuer then holds the Class C tranche, collects the incoming revenues every month, and absorbs any losses themselves.

Asset Classes

Asset classes are different groups of securities which demonstrate characteristics in common, are governed by similar regulations and laws, and behave similarly in the markets. There are five principle classes which include equities (stocks), fixed income (bonds), money market instruments (cash equivalent), commodities (like gold and oil), and real estate (including land, houses, and commercial buildings), as well as some other less common alternative classes of assets.

Many times these different classes of assets are intermingled by financial advisors and analysts. They like these different types of investment vehicles to diversify portfolios more effectively and efficiently. Every asset class is anticipated to provide differing levels and types of risks versus returns among its investment characteristics. They also are supposed to perform differently in any given investment climate. Those investors who seek out the highest possible returns typically do this by lowering their overall portfolio risk by performing diversification of asset classes.

Financial professionals typically focus their clients on the different asset classes as a means of steering them into proper and effective diversification of their investment or retirement portfolios. The various classes of assets possess differing amounts and types of risk as well as varying cash flows. By purchasing into several of the competing asset classes, investors make certain they obtain a proper level of diversification in their investment choices. The importance of diversification can not be overstated. This is because all financial professionals in the know understand that it lowers risk while maximizing the opportunities to earn the highest possible return.

There are a variety of different types of investment strategies available to investors today. They might be associated with value, growth, income, or a combination of some or all of these factors. Each of them works to categorize and label the various investment options per a particular grouping of investment criteria.

There are many analysts who prefer to tie traditional valuation metrics like price to earnings ratios (PE ratios) or growth in earnings per share (EPS) to the investment selection criteria. Still different analysts feel like performance is less of a priority while asset type and allocation are more critical. They know that investments which are in the identical class of assets will possess similar cash flows, returns, and risks.

The most liquid of these various asset classes prove to be equities, fixed income securities, cash- like instruments, and commodities. This also makes them the most frequently quoted, traded, and recommended classes of assets available today. Other asset classes are considered to be more alternative such as real estate, stamps, coins, and artwork, all of which are tradable forms of collectibles. There are also investment choices such as venture capital funds, crowd sourcing, hedge funds, and bitcoin, which are considered to be even more alternative and mostly for sophisticated investors. In general, the rule is that the more alternative the investment turns out to be, the less liquidity it actually possesses.

Some of these investments, such as hedge funds, venture capital funds, and crowd sourcing can take years to exit from, if investors are able to withdraw from the investment at all. Lower liquidity does not necessarily correlate to lower return potential though. It only means that it may be a while before holders are able to find a willing buyer to sell the investments to so they can cash out of the investment.

Many of the most alternative types of investments have boasted among the highest returns over the decades, sometimes significantly better returns than the most popular two asset classes of stocks and bonds. In order to get around this lack of liquidity and often enormous investment capital requirement, many investors choose to utilize REITS. Real Estate Investment Trusts provide greater liquidity while still participating in price appreciation of the real estate asset class.

Asset Protection

Asset Protection and planning refers to strategies and practices for protecting personal wealth. It happens through deliberate and involved planning processes that safeguard individuals' assets from the potential claims of any creditors. Both businesses and individuals alike can employ these specific techniques to reduce the ability of creditors to seize personal or business property within the legal boundaries of creditor debtor law.

What makes Asset Protection so powerful is that it is able to insulate a variety of assets and all legally. It does not require any of the shady or illegal activities inherent in concealing assets, illegal money transferring, bankruptcy fraud, or tax evasion. The asset experts will warn their clients that efficient protection of assets starts in advance of a liability, incident, or claim occurring. The reason is that it is generally over late to begin arranging such protection afterward. There are a wide variety of normal means for protecting such personal or business assets. Among the most popular are family limited partnerships, accounts receivable financing, and asset protection trusts.

In the heavily litigious society of the United States, Asset Protection involves protecting property from those who might win a judgment in court. There are a variety of lawsuits that could threaten a person's or business' assets. Among these are car accident claims, unintentional negligent acts, and even foreclosure on property lawsuits where the mortgage is no longer paid. The ultimate goal in Asset Protection is to take any nonexempt from creditors assets and move them to a position where they become exempt assets beyond the reach of any claims of the various creditors.

Asset Protection which an individual or business does when a lawsuit is already underway or even imminent to be filed will likely be reversed by the courts. This way they can seize the hidden assets that were deliberately transferred to protect them from an imminent court case judgment. This is the ultimate reason why effective protection of assets has to start well in advance of the first hints of litigious activity or creditor claims.

Two principal goals must be combined in order to effectively construct an efficient and ironclad Asset Protection plan. These include achieving both long term and short term goals and reaching estate planning goals. The financial goals component involves clearly understanding present and future income sources, the amount of resources needed for retirement, and any resources which will remain to leave to any heirs via estate planning. This helps people to come up with highly detailed financial plans.

After this has been done, individuals will want to examine carefully any present assets to decide if they are effectively exempted from any and all sundry creditors. The ones that are not should be clearly repositioned so that they are exempt. This also involves planning to position future assets so that they are similarly effectively protected.

The next step is to come up with a complete and all inclusive estate plan. It should encompass all forms of asset protection and relevant planning via advanced techniques of estate planning. Among these are irrevocable trusts for the individuals, their children, spouses, and beneficiaries as well as family limited liability companies.

The most common mistake that people or businesses make with this Asset Protection planning is waiting until it is too late to safeguard the assets. The other mistake is assuming that such planning can be done rapidly or as a short term fix for a longer term problem. Protecting assets is ultimately longer term planning that must be done carefully and ahead of potential creditor claims on assets or pending lawsuits.

Financial Terms Dictionary - Investment Terminology Explained

Cash Savings Account

A cash savings account is a place that you can park your cash and gain interest on it. Effective short term savings accounts are ones that permit you to meet your needs in four important areas. The access to the funds is critical.

Cash savings accounts should allow you to withdraw funds from the account whenever you need. This should be accomplished through convenient methods like ATM cards or online means. Funds in all types of cash savings accounts are insured by the FDIC, or Federal Deposit Insurance Corporation, to $100,000 for all people and $250,000 for retiree accounts.

Interest is another area of concern for cash savings accounts. This pertains to the rate that the bank or institution will give you for holding your money. Larger amounts generally attract superior rates.

Penalties should not have to be endured for withdrawing cash from cash savings accounts either. Certificates of Deposits and other instruments feature such penalties, but cash savings accounts should not. These terms of withdrawal should be clearly specified in any cash savings account.

Finally, service is an issue to be considered with cash savings accounts. You might wish to have customer service in a bank branch included. Otherwise, do it yourself online accounts can be established.

There are several types of cash savings accounts from which you can choose. One is a checking account that includes interest. This might be called a money market account. Such money market accounts include check writing privileges and check based access to funds. These can be held at banks or brokerage houses, which are gaining in popularity at banks' expense. Some privileges besides check writing include higher money market rates of interest and ATM card and machine access to funds. Downsides to these types of accounts include sometimes high minimum balances and possible fees.

Standard savings accounts are another option with cash savings accounts. These were once called passbook accounts. The interest rates provided by these accounts are lower than inflation, which proves to be their major downside. Their major advantage lies in the extremely low account minimums and fees charged to have them.

High yield bank accounts are a third type of cash savings accounts. Providing versatility of adding or withdrawing funds without penalties, they also offer the liquidity of not tying up your money for long periods of time. Nowadays, there are high yield bank accounts that provide interest rates that prove to be comparable to Certificates of Deposits, without showcasing these investments' restrictions on taking out money. The highest rates available on high yield bank accounts come from banks that are online only versions of the traditional lending institutions.

They accomplish this by not offering branches and in person customer service benefits. This means that unless such an online high yield account includes an ATM card, the only way to withdraw the funds is through electronic transfers to other brokerage, savings, or checking accounts, which can result in delays of as much as two to five full days. Without such an ATM card, it can be inconvenient to access cash stored in these accounts in a hurry or emergency situation. High yield accounts sometimes offer shorter term teaser interest rates, so individuals should investigate the product's prior six month history of interest rates to learn what their consistent rates turn out to be.

Certificate of Deposit (CD)

A Certificate of Deposit refers to a kind of savings vehicle which generally provides greater returns for money invested than the typical savings accounts do. There is very little risk in such an account. They also come without monthly fees. Besides this, these CDs prove to be significantly different from the age old savings accounts for several reasons.

Such a Certificate of Deposit stands for a time deposit. While an individual who has a savings account is freely able to make additional deposits or withdraw available funds relatively at will, this is not the case with CDs. Holders of CDs consent to tying up their money for a minimum length of time. Banks calls this the term length. Such term lengths might be only a few days. They could also extend up to ten years out. Standard CD's run from typically three months to five years.

In general, the longer the term length proves to be, the better the rate of interest the Certificate of Deposit will pay. The longer the term length is, the greater amount of time an individual ties up the money in the account at the bank too. It makes sense that the bank rewards customers for committing to a longer amount of time with a larger CD rate than they pay on comparable savings accounts.

Banks generally quote these CD rates using the APY annual percentage yield. This rate takes into account the compounding periods on how often the CD pays interest which can then earn still more interest on it. The banks have the choice of compounding periods based on annually, quarterly, monthly, and daily compounding. The closer a CD compounds to a daily rate, the higher the APY will actually prove to be.

There are penalties involved with drawing the money out of the certificate of deposit before its final maturity date. While every bank is different, most banks will levy a penalty of from three to six months in accrued interest for breaking the time deposit early. This is why financial professionals will counsel against taking money out of a CD early unless it is desperately important to access the funds.

The U.S. FDIC Federal Deposit Insurance Corporation backs the CDs at the overwhelming majority of commercial banks in the country. These

Certificates of Deposit are government guaranteed in amounts of up to $250,000. With the credit union CDs, these certificates become insured by the NCUA National Credit Union Administration for the same maximum amounts. Credit unions which are state-chartered will often utilize private insurance for their CDs. Not any of these forms of insurance cover the penalties for taking out the funds ahead of maturity. Such coverage comes automatically and does not have to be applied for in order for the time deposit to be insured.

There are several different varieties of Certificates of Deposit available. Variable rate CDs are those whose interest rate is connected to the prime interest rate, market indices, Treasury bills rates, or another underlying benchmark. They help depositors to gain from any future point interest rate increases. Callable CDs often include a better rate of interest than a traditional CD. The bank can unilaterally reduce the maturity term period on demand though.

No or low penalty CDs pay lower interest rates but allow investors to more easily obtain their money back from the time deposit without expensive penalties. They often require holders to keep a certain minimum balance in the CD. IRA CDs are traditional certificates of deposit which are contained within an IRA Individual Retirement Account. There are tax advantages and deferrals on taxes of interest payments with these. Finally, Jumbo CDs pay greater rates of interest in exchange for extremely high minimum balances of typically $100,000 and higher.

Collective Investment Fund (CIF)

A collective investment fund is a vehicles that manages a combined group of trust accounts. They are sometimes called collective investment trusts. Trust companies or banks operate these funds. The idea behind them is to pool together the funds and assets of organizations and individuals so that the managers can create bigger and better diversified portfolios.

Two types of these CIFs exist. A1 funds are combined together so that their operators can effectively reinvest or initially invest them. With A2 funds, trusts contribute assets that are not subject to any federal income taxes.

The main goal with a collective investment fund lies in utilizing superior economy of scale in order to reduce costs. The operators are able to combine together pensions and profit sharing funds to come up with a greater amount of assets. Banks then put these funds which are pooled together in a master trust account. The bank that controls the account then serves as executor or trustee of the CIF.

Banks that serve collective investment funds are the fiduciaries. This means that keep the legal title for the fund and all assets within it. The individuals or groups that participate in the CIF still own the results of the invested fund' assets. This makes them the beneficial owners of the relevant assets. Those who are participating within the fund do not actually own any individual assets that the CIF holds. They do maintain an interest in the aggregated assets of the fund.

Banks designed these collective investment funds so that they could improve their investment management tactics. They do this when they pull together a number of accounts' assets and merge them into a single fund with a common investment strategy. Pooling these assets into only one account allows the banks to dramatically reduce their administrative and operating costs for the fund. The investment strategy they come up with is structured to optimize the performance of the investments.

There are a number of different collective investment funds operating. Invesco Trust Company operates several of them. Examples of their funds are the Invesco Balanced Risk Commodity Trust and the Invesco Global Opportunities Trust.

Though comptrollers use the name collective investment funds, other names sometimes refer to these vehicles. Generally applied names for them include common funds, common trust funds, comingled trusts, and collective trusts. An important characteristic of CIFs is that they are not regulated by the Investment Act of 1940 (as with mutual funds) or the SEC Securities Exchange Commission. Instead the OCC Office of the Comptroller of the Currency regulates and oversees them.

Mutual funds and collective investment funds are both pooled funds with an important distinction. These CIFs are not registered investment vehicles. Instead they exist in a class that is similar to hedge funds.

In 1927, the world's first collective fund began. Thanks to the stock market crash that occurred only two years later, CIFs became a scapegoat. They were believed to have contributed to the severe crash. This caused regulators to heavily restrict them. Banks could only provide them to trust clients or by utilizing employee benefit plans. They received a significant boost in the Pension Protection Act of 2006. This act chose them to be the standard option in defined contribution plans. Now 401(k) plans often feature them as an option for stable value.

Commodity Exchange (COMEX)

The COMEX Commodity Exchange is the wholly owned subsidiary of the Chicago Mercantile Group that is responsible for both precious metals and base metals futures and options on futures trading. This once independent exchange is where the speculators, hedging companies, and traders all come to participate in trading FTSE 100 London exchange index options, along with precious metals silver and gold futures and options on futures, and industrial metals futures such as copper, aluminum, lead, and zinc futures.

For the first more than half a century of its existence, the Commodity Exchange proved to be an individually owned and run commodities futures exchange. COMEX arose in New York back in 1933 in the depths of the Great Depression. Through ups and downs in the markets, this exchange endured.

On December 31st of 1974, the Commodity Exchange launched its gold futures contract. This was the date when Americans regained the right to own gold again after a more than 40 year hiatus. This made it the biggest and most important center around the globe for gold futures and options. COMEX next launched options trading based on their gold futures in 1982 to cement their place in the world futures market and history. Silver has also been traded on the exchange since the 1970s.

COMEX merged with rival exchange NYMEX in 1994 to form the two still separately run exchanges under the listing of NYMEX Holdings, Inc. They did not obtain their publicly traded listing on the New York Stock Exchange until November 17th of 2006 when it began to trade under the ticker symbol of NMX. This new entity did not maintain its independence for long.

By March of 2008 the Chicago Mercantile Exchange Group of Chicago had conclusively committed to an agreement to purchase all of NYMEX holdings at a combined stock and cash offering that totaled $11.2 billion. The deal successfully completed in August of 2008.

From this point forward, the once independent and then jointly held NYMEX and COMEX exchanges continued their existence as Designated Contract Markets of the CME Group. As such, they joined the two sister exchanges of the organization, the Chicago Mercantile Exchange and the Chicago Board of Trade. All four of these exchanges together make up the DCMs of the CME Group.

COMEX still maintains its separate identity under the CME Group. The precious metals trade is what it is best known for today. This precious metals complex volume that it transacts both monthly and annually is so large that it is greater than the volume of all competing futures exchanges in the world combined.

Commodities Exchange brings in participation from around the globe. A substantial number of the traders from East Asia, Europe, and the Middle East remain at their offices until the daily closure of COMEX.

This fact provides the Commodities Exchange with unparalleled liquidity almost around the clock. This more or less explains why it has been so very successful for the past near century despite intense competition in a constantly changing global trading environment. The hours that it trades continue to reflect the global participation. This is why the Commodities Exchange has opened ever earlier in order to meet the needs of the Asian, Middle Eastern, and European overseas trading clientele base.

Electronic trading on COMEX starts from the night previously from 4pm until the following morning at 7am. The regular trading session occurs from 8:20am through to 2:30pm. This means that COMEX is open for 21 hours per trading day from Monday to Thursday. Sunday electronic hours begin from 7pm EST. The group publishes both exchange open interest and volume every trading day.

Derivative

In the financial world, derivatives are agreements between two different parties that contain values that are dependent on the price movements of an asset, as anticipated in the future, to which they are linked.

This asset, which might be a currency, stock price, or other element is referred to as the underlying. Derivatives are also alternative investments and financial instruments, of which they are numerous kinds. The most common forms of derivatives are futures, swaps, and options.

Investors use derivatives for many different activities. These include for gaining leverage on an investment so that when a small movement occurs in the value of the underlying, they can realize a great gain in the derivative value.

They may also be employed for speculation to profit from, assuming that the underlying asset value goes in the direction that they anticipate. Businesses might similarly hedge their risks in an underlying through opening a derivative contract that moves conversely to their position in the underlying, canceling all or part of the risk in the process. Investors similarly are capable of gaining exposure to an underlying that does not have a tradable instrument associated with it, like with a weather derivative.

Investors can also utilize derivatives to give themselves the ability to create options in which the derivative value is associated with a particular event or condition being met.

Derivatives principally remain a means of offering hedging insurance, allowing one party to lessen their risk exposure while the other reduces a different kind of risk exposure. Derivatives examples of transferring risk are helpful to consider. Millers and wheat farmers might create a derivative by signing a futures contract. This could specify a certain dollar value of money in exchange for a particular quantity of wheat to be exchanged at a future time. In this case, the two parties have actually diminished their risk for the future. The miller is not exposed to possible shortages of wheat, while the farmer is saved from the possible variances in price.

Risk is not completely eliminated in this example since the derivative contract will not cover events that the contract does not mention in particular, like weather conditions. There is similarly a danger that one of the parties will default on their part of the contract. To mitigate these problems, clearing houses insure many futures contracts, although not every such derivative is insured for the risk of counter party default.

Another way of looking at derivatives in this example is that while they reduce one form of risk, they actually present another one. The miller and farmer both pick up another risk by signing off on this contract. For the farmer, the danger lies in the fact that although he is saved from declines in the price of wheat, he is also exposed to the possibility that wheat prices will rise above the set amount in the contract, costing him extra income that he might have obtained. The miller also picks up a risk that the cost of wheat will drop below the amount that he has locked in with this contract.

Diversifying

Diversifying refers to the means of effectively lowering your investing risk by putting your money into a wide range of various assets. A truly well diversified portfolio offers the benefits of lower amounts of risk than those that are simply invested into one or two asset classes or kinds of investments.

Everyone should engage in some amount of diversification, even if the individual proves to be one who is tolerant of risk. Those individuals who really fear the present day economic uncertainties and very real amounts of risk in the market place will perform better forms of diversification into more asset groups.

Mainstream diversification is always recommended by financial experts because of the common example of not placing all of your investment eggs into just a single basket. If you do have all eggs in the one basket and then drop the basket along the way, then they can all break. The idea is that by placing each egg into its own individual basket, the odds of breaking all of the eggs declines significantly, even if one or several of them do get broken themselves.

Portfolios that have not engaged in diversifying might have only one or two corporations' stocks in them. This proves to be a dangerous investment strategy, since no matter how good a company looks on paper, its stock could decline to as low as zero literally over night. The past few years of the financial collapse have taught many investors the extremely painful lesson that even once blue chip financial companies' stock can decline to practically nothing as they spectacularly collapse.

Any financial expert will confidently state that portfolios made up of a dozen or two dozen varying stocks will have far less chance of plummeting. This becomes even more the case when you pick out stocks from a variety of types, industries, and market capitalization sizes of corporations. Better diversifying in stocks would include some companies that are based in other countries. Diversifying does not simply stop with stocks. It steers investors into bonds, mutual funds, and money market funds as well. Though all of these different investments diversify you, they still leave you mostly exposed to the one currency of the U.S. dollar.

More thorough diversifying will put at least a portion of your investments into assets whose values are not solely expressed in terms of only the American currency. This would include commodities, such as gold, silver, oil, and platinum in particular. Foreign currencies, such as the Euro, Pound, or Swiss Franc are another fantastic means of diversifying, and they can be acquired on the world FOREX exchange in currency accounts.

Real estate, including commercial properties, residential properties, vacation homes, or even real estate investment funds, offers another way to diversify away from U.S. dollar based financial investments such as stocks, bonds, mutual funds, and money market accounts. The strongest diversifying advice is to have at least three to seven completely different investment class vehicles, preferably one or more of which is not denominated in only U.S. dollars.

Dividend

Dividends represent portions of a company's earnings that are returned to the investors in the company's stock. These are typically paid out in cash that is either deposited into the investors' brokerage accounts or can be reinvested directly into the company's stock. As an example of a dividend, every share of Phillip Morris pays around 4.5% dividends on the stock price each year.

Investing in dividend paying stocks is a particular passive income investment strategy that is also a cash flow investment. This passive, or cash flow, income means that you collect income just from holding these stock investments. This kind of strategy entails building up a group of blue chip company stocks that pay large dividend yields which add money to your account usually four times per year, on a quarterly basis. Investors in dividends tremendously enjoy watching these routine deposits in cash arrive in either their bank account, brokerage account, or the mail.

Dividend investors who understand this type of investment are looking for a number of different elements in the stocks that they buy. Such dividend stocks should include a high dividend yield. To qualify as high yields, most value investors prefer to see ones that pay more than do the interest rate yields on U.S. Treasuries. Dividend yields can be easily determined. All that you have to do is to take the amount of the dividend and divide it by the price of the stock. So a stock that offers a $2 dividend and costs $40 is paying a five percent dividend yield.

Dividend paying stocks should also feature high dividend coverage. This coverage simply refers to the safety of a dividend, or how likely it is to be reduced or even eliminated. Companies that earn their profits from a large array of businesses are more likely to be able to continue paying their dividends than are companies that make all of their money off of a single business that could be threatened.

A more tangible way of expressing the coverage lies in how many times the dividend total dollar amount is covered by the corporation's total earnings. A company with fifty million dollars in profits that pays twenty million in dividends has its dividend covered by two and a half times. Should their profits drop by ten percent or more, they will have no trouble still paying the same dividend amount to shareholders. The dividend payout ratio is another way of measuring this. On the above example it would be forty percent. Dividend investors prefer to see no more than sixty percent of profits given out as dividends, as this could signify that the company lacks future opportunities for growth and expansion.

Qualified dividends are a third element that dividend investors are looking for in their dividend paying stocks. This simply means that stocks that are kept for less than a year do not benefit from lower tax rates on dividends. Since the government is attempting to convince you to become a longer term investor, you should take advantage of these lower tax rates by only buying stocks with qualified dividends that you have held for a full year and more.

Dividend Yield

Dividend yield refers to the payout of dividend price ratio on a given company's stock. It is simply determined by taking the yearly dividend payment total and dividing it by the cost for each share. This dividend yield is commonly given out as a percentage. The reciprocal of dividend yield proves to be the price to dividend ratio.

Dividend yields vary depending on whether a stock is a preferred stock or a common stock. With preferred shares, these dividend yields are outlined specifically in the stock's prospectus. A company will generally call such a preferred class of stock by the name first given to it, which included the yield based on this initial price. This might be a five percent preferred share. Since the pricing of preferred stock shares go up and down with the dictates of the market, the current yield will vary with the changes in price.

Preferred share holders have a variety of yields that they can figure up. These depend on the eventual disposition of their preferred share security. Besides the current yield formula of amount of dividend per price of preferred share, there are present value yields and a yield to maturity. These other yields only apply to those investors who purchase preferred stock shares after they have been issued or who choose to hold them until the reach the stated maturity date.

Preferred share dividends are almost always higher than the dividend yields on common stock shares.

Common stock shares have a dividend yield that differs entirely. With such common shares, the dividend amount is not guaranteed, and could vary from one quarter to the next. These dividends that are given to you, the common stock holder, are determined by the company's management. As such, they depend on the earnings of the company for the given quarter.

With common stocks, you can not be assured that dividends will be paid in the future that match dividends paid previously, or that these dividends will be paid period. Since it proves to be so challenging to correctly predict future dividends, the figures used in determining dividend yields are the present dividend yields. This means that the present dividend yield is always determined by dividing the most current full year's dividend by the present share price.

Dividend yields can have a major impact on how much money a stock makes for its owners over time. Dr. Jeremy Siegel is a well respected professor of investments who has determined conclusively with his research that ninety-nine percent of all after inflation gains that investors realize with stocks come from only dividends that are reinvested. Reinvestment of dividends means that the dividend yield amounts are simply taken and used to purchase more shares of the stock, instead of paying them out as cash to the share holder's account. This allows for investors to compound the number of shares that they own in a company over time.

Exchange Traded Funds (ETF)

These ETF's prove to be stock market exchange traded investment funds that work very much like stocks. Exchange Traded Funds contain instruments like commodities, stocks, and bonds. They trade for around the identical net asset value as the assets that they contain throughout the course of a day. The majority of ETF's actually follow the value of an index like the Dow Jones Industrial or the S&P 500. Since their creation in 1993, ETF's have evolved into the most beloved kind of exchange traded instruments.

The first Exchange Traded Fund particular to countries proved to be a joint venture of MSCI, Funds Distributor, and BGI. This first product finally turned into the iShares name that is accepted and recognized all over earth today. In the first fifteen years, such ETF's were index funds that simply followed indexes. The United States Securities and Exchange Commission began allowing firms to establish actively managed ETF's back in 2008.

Exchange Traded Funds provide a number of terrific advantages for smaller investors. Among these are elements like simple and effective diversification, index funds tax practicality, and expense ratios that remain very low. While doing all of this, they also offer the appeal of familiarity for you who trade stocks. This includes such comfortable and helpful options as limit orders, options, and short selling the ETF's. Since it is so inexpensive to purchase, hold, and sell these ETF's, many investors in ETF shares choose to keep them over a longer time frame for purposes of diversification and asset allocation. Still other investors trade in and out of these instruments regularly in order to participate in their strategies for market timing investing.

Exchange Traded Funds boast of many advantages. On the one hand, they provide great flexibility in buying and selling. It is easy for you to sell and buy them at the actual market price any time during a trading day, in contrast to mutual funds that you can only acquire at a trading day's conclusion. Since they are companies that trade like stocks, you can buy them in margin accounts and sell them short, meaning that they can be used for hedging purposes too. ETF's also allow limit orders and stop loss orders, which are helpful for assuring entry prices and protecting profits or safeguarding from losses.

ETF's also provide lower costs for traders. This results from the majority of ETF's not being actively managed. Also, ETF's do not spend large amounts of money on distribution, marketing, and accounting costs. The majority of them do not have the fees associated with most mutual funds either.

ETF's are among the greatest vehicles for diversifying portfolios quickly and easily. As an example, with only one set of shares, you can "own" the entire S&P 500 index. ETF's will give you exposure to country specific indexes, international markets, commodities, and even bond indexes.

ETF's have two other advantages. They are both transparent and tax efficient. Transparent in this regard means that they are clear in their portfolio holdings and are priced all day long. They are tax efficient as they do not create many capital gains, since they are not in the business of buying and selling their underlying indexes. They also are not required to sell their holding in order to meet redemptions of investors.

Futures Contracts

Futures contracts are legally binding agreements which two parties usually enter into on a futures exchange trading floor or electronic platform. They spell out the particulars for selling or buying specific financial instruments or commodities for a pre-set price at an exact moment in the future. Such contracts have become standardized to make it easy to trade them on the various futures exchanges. They provide information on the quantity and quality of the commodity, though this depends on the nature of the underlying asset.

Futures contracts can be settled in two ways. Some of them require actual physical delivery of the commodity specified. Others simply settle between the two parties in cash. These contracts specify all important characteristics for the item which the parties are trading. This makes them different from the word "futures" that more generally refers to the markets in which these commodities and instruments trade.

There are two actual types of participants in the futures markets who utilize such futures contracts. These are speculators and hedgers. Individual traders and managers of portfolios can use them to place speculative bets on the direction of price movements for the given asset that underlies the contracts. Hedgers involve buyers or producers of the contact asset itself attempting to lock in the price for which they will later buy or sell their commodity.

There are many different commodities and assets for which futures contracts exist. The most obvious of these are hard assets such as precious metals, industrial metals, natural gas, crude oil and other energy products, grains, seeds, livestock, oils, and carbon credits. Literally dozens of the more significant stock market indices around the globe have these contracts available to trade. Some major individual stocks have their own futures contract on their shares as well. The major interest rates and most important currency pairs also have such contracts and markets to trade.

Futures contracts which require physical delivery do not often result in such physical delivery. Many investors in these contracts trade them and sell them before the date of delivery. They can roll them forward by selling the imminent to expire contract and buying a further month out to replace them.

For producers of a good, these contracts provide a unique solution to the problem of fluctuating prices. Oil producers are classic examples. They might intend to produce a million barrels of oil to deliver in precisely a year. If the price is $50 for a barrel today, and the producer does not want to risk prices falling lower, it could lock it in. Oil prices have become so volatile that they could be substantially lower or higher a year from now. By selling a futures contract, the producer gives up the opportunity to possibly sell the oil for more in a year. It also eliminates the risk of receiving a lower amount.

Mathematical models actually determine the prices of futures contracts. They consider the present day spot price, time until maturity, risk free return rates, dividends, dividend yields, convenience yields, and storage costs. This might mean with oil prices at $50 that a one year futures contract sells for $53. The producer receives a guarantee for $53 million and will have to provide the 1 million barrels of oil on the exact delivery date. It will obtain this $53 per barrel price despite the spot prices at which the markets are trading on that date.

Gold Roth IRA

Gold Roth IRA's are IRA's that are allowed to contain gold and other precious metals. Gold Roth IRA's make sense for many investors. This is because gold and other precious metals like silver and platinum have been considered to be the greatest form of long term storage for cash and valuables throughout history.

This means that gold in particular could be considered to be the best asset for retirement. Although there are many other types of instruments used for retirement accounts and planning, including bonds, stocks, savings, and annuities, gold is the only one whose final value does not rest on an institution or individual's performance or success. This makes physical gold an ideal means for saving for retirement.

Gold Roth IRA's are specially created either through initially funding one or by rolling over a Roth IRA or traditional IRA to a gold backed Roth IRA. Rolling over an existing employee held 401K to a Gold Roth IRA can be difficult if the employee has not left the company. This is because employees are not usually allowed to do rollovers until they separate from their company.

IRA's that already exist can be transferred to Gold Roth IRA's. They can be moved from credit unions, banks, or stock broker firms to a trust company that is allowed to hold your Gold IRA holdings. In this type of transfer, you could choose to move securities held in the account along with cash, or cash by itself.

Gold Roth IRA's must be created by sending in cash to the administrator of the IRA. They will then purchase the gold, silver, or platinum physical holdings as you instruct them. The gold must then be kept by a gold IRA custodian on your behalf. These depositories provide safe places for the gold, as well as easy access to buy or sell it. The gold kept in a Gold Roth IRA may not be sent to your house or assumed in your personal possession. Instead, it has to be liquidated before the funds from it can be accessed. Gold that is requested as a distribution will be penalized at your personal tax rate plus a ten percent penalty.

Only certain forms of gold and precious metals are allowed to be purchased and held within a Gold Roth IRA. Gold bars have to demonstrate a twenty-four karat purity to be eligible. They can be one ounce, ten ounces, a kilogram, one hundred ounces, or four hundred ounces in size. Gold coins that are permitted are twenty-four karat bullion coins from the United States, Canada, Austria, and Australia. The most heavily minted gold coins of all time, the South Africa Krugerrand's, are not permitted, as they are only twenty-two karats.

Silver bars and coins that have .999 or higher purity are permitted to be held in a Gold Roth IRA account. This allows the Canadian Silver Maple Leaf, the U.S. Silver Eagle, and the Mexican Silver Libertad one ounce bullion coins. Silver bars that are one hundred ounces and one thousand ounces are also permitted.

Government Bonds

Government bonds are debt instruments that governments issue to pay for government expenditures. Within the United States, federal government issues include savings bonds, treasury notes, treasury bonds, and TIPS Treasury inflation protected securities. Investors should carefully consider the risks that different countries' governments possess before they invest in their bonds. Among these international government risks are political risk, country risk, interest rate risk, and inflation risk. Governments generally have less credit risk, though not always.

Savings bonds are a type of United States government bonds that the Treasury department sells. They are available in an electronic form. The Treasury offers them directly from their website, or individuals can buy them from the majority of financial institutions and banks. When savings bonds reach maturity, the investors get back the bond's face value along with interest which accrued. These savings bonds may not be redeemed the first year of issue. Any investors who redeem them in their first five years of issue lose three months interest for cashing out too early.

The Treasury of the United States also issues intermediate time frame bonds known as Treasury notes or T-Notes. These notes provide interest payments semiannually at a coupon rate which is fixed. These notes typically are denominated in $1,000 face values. Those with three or two year maturity dates come in $5,000 denominations. Before 1984, T-Notes were callable and gave the Treasury the right to buy them back given specific conditions.

The U.S. government's longest term bonds are Treasury Bonds, or T-Bonds. These have maturity dates ranging from ten to 30 years time. They also provide interest payments on a semiannual basis and come in $1,000 denominated values. These T-bonds are important because they pay for federal budget shortfalls, are a form of monetary policy, and ensure the country is able to regulate its money supply. As all bond issuers, the Treasury department looks at return and risk requirements on the market when it goes to raise capital so that it can be as efficient as possible. This helps to explain the different kinds of Treasury securities and government bonds they offer.

U.S. government bonds have generally been considered to be without risk, which is why they trade so easily in extremely large and liquid markets. The downside to this is that they offer considerably lower returns than do other bonds. TIPS do provide protection against inflation so that any inflation increases will not exceed the interest rate of the bond. The prices of government bonds are based on current interest rates. This means that the fixed rate bonds will decline in value as the interest rates rise, since there is lost opportunity to obtain newer bonds at higher interest rates. Similarly, if interest rates fall, the bond's values will rise.

The federal government is able to control the money supply in part by its issue of the government bonds. If they wish to increase the money supply, they can simply buy back their own bonds. These funds then find their way to a bank and expand the money supply as banks keep small reserves and loan the rest out (in the money multiplier effect). The government is also able to lower the money supply by selling additional bonds which takes money out of circulation. If the government were to retire the funds received from the sale of these bonds, it would reduce the available money supply. More often than not, the U.S. government spends the money.

High Frequency Trading (HFT)

High frequency trading turns out to be a platform for program-based trades. It works with super computers that are able to run huge quantities of trading orders at incredibly rapid speeds. This HFT works with complicated algorithms. These analyze a wide range of markets and then place a number fast-paced orders depending on the conditions in the markets. The secret of the trading algorithms lies in their speed. Those traders who have the quickest trade executions usually make more money than do traders who have slower trade executions.

This high frequency trading has not always been mainstream or even possible. It grew in popularity as some of the exchanges began to provide incentives for corporations that could increase the stock market's liquidity.

As an example, the NYSE New York Stock Exchange works with a number of liquidity providers. These are known as SLPs Supplemental Liquidity Providers. The strive to provide better liquidity and more competition for the exchange and its already existing quotes.

The companies that participate in this program earn either a rebate or a fee when they increase the liquidity. This amount turned out to be $0.0019 in mid 2016 for securities that are listed on the NYSE or NYSE MKT. It may not sound like an enormous amount of money. It adds up to major profits quickly as some of these companies are engaged in millions of transactions on busy days.

The NYSE and other exchanges introduced this SLP program for a specific reason. After Lehman Brothers collapsed back in 2008, liquidity turned into an enormous concern for market participants. The SLP provided the solution to low liquidity. It also made high frequency trading a major part of the stock market in only a few years.

High frequency trading offers some significant benefits to the stock exchanges and financial markets. The most significant one centers on the significantly better liquidity that the programs provide. It has reduced bid ask spreads substantially. Larger spreads are more or less a thing of the past.

Some exchanges tested the benefits by trying to place fees on the HFT. The spreads then increased as fewer trades occurred. The Canadian government started charging fees for high frequency trading on Canadian markets. A study concluded that the end result was 9% higher bid to ask spreads.

There are many who dislike high frequency trading as well. Opponents are harsh in their criticism. Many broker dealers have been eliminated by the computer programs. The human element has been removed from many decisions on the exchanges.

When errors occur, the critics are quick to point out that human interactions could have prevented them. Part of the problem in the speed is that the programs are making decisions in literally thousandths of a second. This can lead to huge moves in the market with no apparent explanation or reason.

The best example of the mistakes that can lead to enormous and scary stock market moves happened on May 6, 2010 during the Flash Crash. The DJIA Dow Jones Industrial Average experienced its biggest drop of all time on an intraday basis. The Dow plunged over 1,000 points and dropped a full 10% in only twenty minutes. It then recovered back much of the loss in the next few hours. When the government investigated the issue, they found an enormous order which had caused the sell off to begin. The HFT computer algorithms did all the rest.

Another criticism concerns large corporate profiting at the expense of the smaller retail investors. The trade off is superior liquidity. Unfortunately, much of this turns out to be phantom liquidity. It is there for the market at one moment and then gone in another. This keeps the traders from benefiting from the liquidity.

Individual Retirement Account (IRA)

An IRA stands for Individual Retirement Account. IRA's offer two types of savings for retirement. They can either be tax free or tax deferred retirement plans. In the universe of IRA's, numerous different types of accounts exist. These are principally either traditional and standard IRA's or Roth IRA's as the most popular types. The various IRA's are helpful to different individuals based on the particular scenarios and end goals of every person.

Standard IRA's permit contributions of as much as $4,000 every year. These are contributions that are tax deductible, giving the IRA's their primary advantage as retirement accounts. People who are older than fifty are allowed to contribute more than the $4,000 maximum for the purposes of catching up for their approaching retirement. Any money put into the IRA is used to reduce your annual income amount, which lessens your overall tax liability for the year.

The tax is really only deferred though, since monies taken from an IRA will be taxed at the typical income tax rate for the individual when they are withdrawn, even if they are held in such an account until retirement. When the money is taken out earlier than this age of 59 ½, then an extra ten percent penalty is applied as well. There are exceptions to the penalty rule though. When these early withdrawn monies are utilized to buy a home or to pay for the tuition costs associated with higher education, then they are not penalized. The typical tax rate would still apply, although the penalty is waived in these two cases. This makes IRA's a good vehicle for investments that also give you the versatility of making significant purchases with the money.

Roth IRA's are the other principal type of IRA's. The government established these types of IRA account back in 1997 in an effort to assist those Americans in the middle class with their retirement needs. Roth IRA's do not turn out to be tax deductible. The upside is that they offer greater amounts of flexibility than do the typical IRA's. These contributions are allowed to be taken out whenever you want without a penalty or extra tax. Interest that the account earns is taxed if taken out before the first five years have passed. At the end of five years, the earnings and contributions both made are capable of being taken out without having to pay either taxes or penalties. The identical housing and education allowances that permit to standard IRA's pertain to Roth IRA's. The principal attraction of Roth IRA's is that they offer tax free income at retirement time.

It is worth noting that the Roth IRA's have their particular rules that keep them from being for everybody. If your income is higher than $95,000 in a year, then you will be barred from making the full contribution, and if it exceeds $110,000, then you will not be allowed to make a partial contribution. For married, filing jointly, the limits are $150,000 for full contributions and $160,000 for partial contributions.

Intraday

Intraday refers to trades that occur during the normal course of the day. These price movements are especially important for traders who practice short term trading. They attempt to earn profits trading repeatedly throughout the one day trading session. Sometimes the term is utilized to refer to securities which engage in normal trading on the stock exchanges throughout the regular hours' session. This would include ETFs exchange traded funds and company stocks.

On the other hand, investors must purchase mutual funds from dealers directly. Their transactions typically occur after the stock market exchanges close for the day. This happens because the mutual funds must calculate their closing NAV Net Asset Value before they can lock in the buying and selling prices for their fund shares each market day.

Intraday also can be employed to explain a new low or high for a given security. It is always illuminating to consider a real example of such concepts. When dealers or analysts refer to a new Intraday low, they signify that the security touched a new low as compared to its other price points throughout the day in a single trading session. There are many cases where such an intraday low or high is the same as the final closing price for the given security.

Short term traders are always interested in these single day price movements. They watch them carefully with computer power-generated real time charts. This helps them to ascertain the right points to trade in and out in an effort to make money on the short term volatility and movements in the underlying issue stock prices. These shorter term time frame traders generally deploy 60, 30, 15, five, and one minute charts as they are trading in a single session and day. They might employ the five and one minute charts for scalping, while they would utilize the 60 and 30 minute charts for holding periods of a longer several hours.

There are a range of advantages and disadvantages to such Intraday trading. The greatest benefit to it lies in the fact that any unforeseen after market news can not impact the prices of the securities themselves. As an example, consider a surprise earnings report or important economic data release. There are also broker downgrades and upgrades which might happen after the market has closed or before it even opens. By only trading stocks on a throughout the day basis, short term and scalping traders avoid these pitfalls which can cause dramatic price swings and shocks. Intraday trading also permits tighter stop loss orders, greater opportunities for learning, and higher leverage limitations.

Disadvantages in such trading are that there is not always enough time for various stock prices to gain sufficiently in profit. Commission costs are also significantly higher as the traders on a short term basis are often in and out of positions repeatedly throughout he day, raising the costs of trading.

Short term traders are not without their effective strategies that help them to realize profits on an intraday basis. Some of them are range trading in which they work off of resistance and support levels in order to decide sell and buy entry and exit points. There are also scalping trades that seek to earn a large number of profits on minute changes in the price of the securities in question. News-based trading seeks to gain advantage on the increased volatility levels surrounding announced news which may make for interesting and exciting trading opportunities on an intraday basis. Finally, there are high frequency trading strategies. These employ expensive and complicated computer algorithms to take advantage of tiny inefficiencies in the single day trading markets.

Intrinsic Value

Intrinsic value has several meanings where finance and business are concerned. The first of these meanings pertains to companies and their underlying stock issues. An intrinsic value of a stock could be said to be the actual per share value of a stock, in contrast to its book value or price according to the stock market.

Intrinsic value takes many other elements into account, such as trademarks and copyrights owned, as well as the value of the brand name. These factors are intangible in nature. This makes it hard to figure out their true worth, although it can be done. As a result of this, such items of intrinsic value are not commonly included in the stock's actual market price.

A different way of understanding intrinsic value is that the intrinsic value is the amount that a company is actually worth. Market capitalization on the other hand is the price that investors will willingly pay for a company at any given point. Intrinsic value can be calculated in varying ways, depending on the investor who is doing the calculation.

Intrinsic value is also the amount of money that a call or put option on a stock is in the money. Call options give investors the right but not the obligation to buy a stock at a certain price, while put options grant investors the right but not obligation to sell a stock at a particular price. Figuring up a call option's intrinsic value is done by simply taking the difference of the call option's strike price and subtracted from the actual price of the underlying stock.

As an example, a call option might have a strike price of $40. The stock that this option is based on could be worth $55 per share. This would give the option an intrinsic value of $15 each share, or $1,500 since stock options represent a hundred shares. Stock prices that prove to be lower than call options do not possess any intrinsic value.

Put option intrinsic values are found by taking the difference of the strike price of the put option and subtracting the price of the stock that underlies them. As an example, should a put option contain a strike price of $30, and the stock be trading at only $25, then the put option will have an intrinsic value of $5 per share, or $500 for the one hundred share option. On the other hand, if the stock market price turned out to be higher than the strike price of this put option, then the option would not contain any intrinsic value.

Intrinsic value is also the true, real worth of an asset or object. Gold and silver have intrinsic value in that people will pay you for them at any time and in any country. Conversely, paper currencies may only be said to have intrinsic value if they are linked to or backed up by a hard asset.

Investment Value

Investment Value refers to an asset's specific value given a particular range of investment parameters. It can be defined as the property value to a given group of investors (or an individual investor) who have specific investment goals in mind. This makes it a subjective measurement of the asset or property's value.

Many times potential investors will employ the investment value metric when they have an interest in buying a certain real estate property with a particular group of investment goals and objectives. It might be they have a targeted return rate they are looking for in the investment. This is why such a value metric heavily involves motivations and beliefs in a particular investment strategy.

The reason that this investment value would have importance on a transaction concerns buyers contemplating buying a given asset when they want to compare the pricing of the real estate or asset in question to the anticipated rate of return. When they are able to use this value to consider their specific rate of return, they are able to measure up the investment final results with the projected price they will pay out for the property. This helps them to make an intelligent purchasing decision consistent with their investment objectives.

In contrast to the investment value, market value is the true value of the property (or asset) in question based on the supply and demand of the open market. It is typically determined by utilizing the appraisal process where Real Estate is concerned. This contrasts with the individual investors' value they may place on the property as it pertains to their unique goals, objectives, and needs for the property they are considering.

It is important to realize that investment value is not the same as market value in many cases. The investment values might be lower, higher, or the same to the market values. This would heavily depend on the property's specific scenario at the time. In fact the market values and investing values are typically approximately the same. Yet they can diverge.

For example, investment value might be greater than that of the market value. A certain buyer may place a higher value on the property than would a typical informed purchaser. This could happen in the real world when a firm decides to expand its premises into a larger newer building that has just gone on sale across the road from the current company offices. The company might be willing to pay a higher price than the market value so that it could ensure competitors stay out of the market and do not secure the building before they can conclude the transaction. In such a scenario, this extra value becomes derived from the strategic advantage that the firm will realize by having the property.

Where a single investor is concerned, it is also possible for investment value to exceed the market value. An example of this could be when the investors have a special tax status or situation that can not be transferred. They might also have some type of highly advantageous financing terms that do not apply to rival investors or buyers.

It is similarly possible for investment value to be under that of the market value on a property. This could happen when the given property is not a kind in which the investors normally specialize or concentrate their efforts. As an example, for multifamily developers, choosing to consider developing a hotel could cause the investment value for this particular situation to be lower than the traditional market value for the given site. This would be because of the greater costs involved in learning to develop the property. It might also be that the investors are seeking out and demand a higher than average return from a property thanks to their current portfolio diversification and allocation.

Leverage

Where business and finance are concerned, leverage pertains to the concept of using investment capital, revenue, or equity to multiply any gains or losses realized. Leverage can be affected in various ways. Among the most popular means of achieving it are through purchasing fixed assets, borrowing money, or utilizing derivatives.

There are several important examples to the use of leverage. With investments, hedge funds work with derivatives to leverage their capital. They could do this by putting up one million dollar cash for their margin and using it to control twenty million dollars of crude oil. They then realize any and all gains or losses achieved by the twenty million dollar crude position.

Businesses may similarly achieve leverage on their revenue by purchasing fixed assets. In so doing, the business would boost its proportion of fixed costs. Any change in revenue would then lead to a greater change in the associated operating income.

Publicly traded corporations are also able to obtain leverage on their stock share holder equity through borrowing money. The greater amount of cash that they borrow, the lower amount of equity capital they will require. This translates to all profits and losses being distributed out to a smaller share holder base, making them proportionately bigger in the end.

There are formulas for the four main types of leverage. Accounting leverage is found by taking all assets and dividing them by all assets minus all liabilities. Notional leverage is found by taking all notional quantities of assets, adding them to all of the notional liabilities, and then dividing the result by equity. To find the economic leverage, the equity volatility has to be divided by the identical assets' unlevered investment volatility. Finally, operating leverage can be calculated through taking the revenue in question and subtracting out the variable cost, then dividing the operating income into the result.

Leverage entails significant benefits and also substantial risks. While it does allow potentially great amounts of money to be made when investments go the way of an individual or organization, it can also involve devastating losses when the investments move against the entity. As an example, a stock investor who purchases stocks with fifty percent margin will double his losses when a stock goes down. Companies that borrow excessively to increase their leverage can experience collapse and bankruptcy in a downturn in business at the same time as a company with less leverage could survive.

Not all uses of leverage entail the same degree of risk. Corporations that borrow money so that they can engage in international expansion, increase their line up of products, or modernize their plants and equipment gain additional diversification. This could provide more than just an offset for the extra risks that result from the leverage. Not all highly leveraged companies are risky either. Public utilities commonly include high levels of debt, but they are generally considered to be less risky than are technology companies that lack leverage.

Mortgage Broker

A mortgage broker is a firm or sole proprietorship that performs a role as an intermediary between banks and businesses or individuals who are looking for mortgage loans. Even though banks have always vended their own mortgage products, mortgage brokers have gradually taken a larger and larger share of the loan originating market as they seek out direct lenders and banks that have the specific products that a customer wants or needs.

Nowadays, sixty-eight percent of all loans begin with mortgage brokers in the United States, making them by far and away the biggest vendors of mortgage products for banks and lenders. The remaining thirty-two percent of loans come from banks own direct marketing efforts and retail branch efforts. Mortgage broker fees are separate from the bank mortgage fees. They are based on the loans' amounts themselves and range from commonly one to three percent of the total loan amount.

Mortgage brokers are mostly regulated in order to make sure that they comply with finance laws and banking rules in the consumer's jurisdiction. This level of regulation does vary per state. Forty-nine of the fifty states have their own laws or boards that regulate mortgage lending within their state's borders. The industry is similarly governed by ten different federal laws that are applied by five federal agencies for enforcement.

Banks find mortgage brokers to be an ideal means of bringing in borrowers who will qualify for a loan. In this way, a mortgage broker acts as a screening agent for a bank. Banks are furthermore able to shift forward a portion of the fraud and foreclosure risks to the loan originators using their contractual legal arrangements with them. In the originating of a loan, a mortgage broker will do the footwork of collecting and processing all of the necessary paper work associated with real estate mortgages.

Mortgage brokers should not be confused with loan officers of a bank. Mortgage brokers are typically state registered and also licensed in order to work as a mortgage broker. This makes them liable personally for any fraud that they commit during the entire life span of the loans in question. Being a mortgage broker comes with professional, legal, and ethical responsibilities that include proper disclosure of mortgage terms to consumers.

Mortgage brokers come with all kinds of experience, as do loan officers, who are employees of banks. While loan officers commonly close more loans than mortgage brokers actually do because of their extensive network of referrals within the bank for which they work, the majority of mortgage brokers make more money than loan officers make. Mortgage brokers generate the lion's share of all loan originations within the country as well.

Mortgage brokers are all represented by the NAMB, which is the acronym for their group the National Association of Mortgage Brokers. The NAMB's mission is to represent the industry of mortgage brokers throughout the U.S. It also offers education, resources to members, and a certification program as well.

Municipal Bonds

Municipal bonds prove to be counties', cities', and states' debt obligations. They issue these in order to raise money against future tax revenues for building highways, schools, sewer systems, hospitals, and numerous other public welfare projects.

When you as an investor buy a municipal bond, you are actually loaning a state or local government or agency money. They agree to pay you back your principal, along with a certain sum of interest that is generally paid out twice a year. The principal is commonly given back on the pre arranged maturity date of the bond.

The advantage that is most commonly touted to municipal bonds is their tax free nature. The truth is that not every municipal bond actually provides income which is tax free on both state and federal levels. Many municipal bond issues are exempt from taxes from the state and local authorities but still have to pay taxes on earning to the federal government. Municipal bonds that come without any federal taxes as well are generally known as Munis. These Munis prove to be the most appealing bonds for many investors since they are generally exempt from all Federal, state, and local taxes too. Besides this, Munis are commonly investments made in the local and state infrastructure, impacting your daily quality of life and that of your community. Projects including highways, hospitals, and housing are all covered by these types of municipal bonds.

Municipal bonds can also be further subdivided into one of two general categories. These are general obligation bonds and revenue bonds. With a general obligation bond, the interest and principal that is owed to you is commonly backed up by the issuer's own credit and faith. They typically come underpinned by the taxing power of the issuer. This can be based on their limited or unlimited powers of taxing. General obligation bonds usually come approved by the voters who will pay the taxes that support their repayment.

Revenue bonds on the other hand are backed up by specific revenues for the project in question. Their interest and principal payment amounts have supporting revenues that come from tolls, rents from the facility that they build, or charges to use the facility that is built. Many different public works are built with revenue bonds. These could be airports, bridges, roads, sewage and water treatment plants, subsidized housing, and even hospitals. A great number of such bonds come issued by authorities which are specifically launched to create such bond issues in the first place.

Municipal bonds and notes commonly come with minimum investment amounts. These are typically denominated by $5,000. They can come in multiples of $5,000 increments as well. If you want to buy a municipal bond, you can buy them directly off of the bond issuer when they come out on the primary market, or alternatively off of other bond holders after they have come out, from the secondary market.

Mutual Funds

Mutual funds prove to be collective investment pools that are managed professionally. They derive their sometimes enormous capitals from the contributions of many different investors. These monies are then invested in a variety of investments and securities comprised of bonds, stocks, other mutual funds, money markets, and commodities like silver and gold.

Mutual funds all have a fund manager. His responsibility is to sell and buy the holdings of the fund according to the guidelines spelled out in the particular mutual fund's prospectus. U.S. regulations require that all mutual funds registered with the governing SEC, or Securities and Exchange Commission, make distributions of practically all income and net gains made from selling securities to the investors minimally once a year. The majority of these mutual funds are furthermore overseen by trustees or boards of directors. Their job is to make certain that the fund is properly managed by its investment adviser for the investors of the funds ultimate good.

There are really a wide variety of different securities that mutual funds are permitted by the SEC to purchase. This is somewhat limited by the objectives spelled out in the prospectus of the fund, which is comprised of a great amount of useful information on the fund and its goals. While cash instruments, stocks, and bonds are the more common types of investments that they purchase, mutual funds might also buy exotic types of investments like forwards, swaps, options, and futures.

The investment objectives of mutual funds explain clearly the types of investments that the fund will purchase. As an example, if a fund's objective claimed that it was attempting to realize capital appreciation through investing in U.S. company stocks regardless of their amount of market capitalization, then it would be a U.S. stock fund that purchased U.S company stocks.

Other mutual funds purchase specific market sectors or different industries. Utilities, technology, and financial service funds are examples of this. Such a fund is called a sector fund or specialty fund. There are also bond funds that purchase different kinds of bonds, like investment grade corporate bonds or high yield junk bonds. They can invest in the bonds issued by government agencies, municipalities, or companies.

They might also be divided up according to whether they purchase long term or short term maturities of bonds. These funds may also buy bonds or stocks of either domestic companies or global companies, or even international companies outside of the United States. Index funds are another type of mutual fund that attempts to match a certain market index's performance over time. The S&P 500 index is an example of one on which index mutual funds are based. With this type of index fund, the mutual fund would find derivatives based on the S&P 500 stock index futures so that they could match the index's performance as identically as possible.

To help investors better understand the type of fund that they are getting into, the SEC came out with a particular name rule in the 40' Act that makes funds actually invest in minimally eighty percent of securities that actually match up with their name. So a fund called the New York Tax Free Bond Fund would have to use eighty percent or more of its funds to purchase investments of tax free bonds that New York State and its various agencies issued.

Mutual Funds Dividends

Where mutual funds are concerned, dividends are quite different than they turn out to be for stocks. Mutual fund dividends are actually required distributions of both income as well as capital gains that are realized that have to be paid out to investors in mutual funds.

Mutual funds often bring in varying types of income. The challenge lies in the fact that all of these incomes come with varying tax treatments. In the majority of cases, such differences in taxes are passed through to the investors in the mutual fund. As an example, should a mutual fund own a stock for longer than a single year and then sell it to realize a capital gain, then a portion of the investors' mutual fund dividends would be classified as a long term capital gain. This would permit you to realize the advantages of such types of income's lower tax rates.

There are varying types of dividends paid out by mutual funds. One of these is ordinary dividends. These cover every type of taxable income besides the long term capital gains. This does not mean that they are always treated as ordinary tax rate income, since some of these dividends will be qualified dividends that receive preferential tax rate treatment.

Some of the distributions that come from your mutual fund could be long term capital gains. These do get the better form of tax treatment. Shorter term capital gains in these funds are generally distributed along with the regular dividends.

Some mutual funds buy into state or local government debts or municipal bonds. This results in a portion of your mutual fund distributions being treated as interest that is tax exempt. These interest payments might still impact social security benefits though, so it is wise to consult a tax professional concerning them.

Should your mutual fund be investing money into the Federal Government's debt obligations, then these distributions can often be treated as interest paid by the federal government. Such income is not given favorable Federal income tax treatment. It does become exempt from state income types of taxation.

From time to time, mutual funds will issue payments that are not income at all. This is a non dividend distribution. All that it represents is a portion of the money that was invested by you in the first place being returned to you. These distributions usually do not even have to be reported. They must be used in determining the amount of loss or gain incurred when you sell the mutual fund shares, though.

A final mutual fund dividend paid out is a capital gain allocation. These are highly unusual, since the overwhelming majority of mutual funds do capital gain distributions instead. While it is highly uncommon to see such a capital gain allocation, if you do get one, then you will have to use the special Form 2439 that your mutual fund sends to you in dealing with the particular tax rules.

MyRA Account

MyRA Account is a new form of retirement plan that the government set up under the auspices of the U.S. Department of the Treasury. They intended it for workers who do not have access to any other form of retirement plan through their workplace and who do not have a convenient vehicle of their own for saving for retirement. It is a Roth IRA and is governed by the Roth IRA rules.

It offers several advantages other forms of retirement accounts do not. There are no fees or costs to set it up or maintain it. The account is automatically invested in a government Treasury fund and pays the simple rate, so there are not any complex investment options or decisions to make. Because it is based in Treasuries of the United States government, there is no risk of losing any money. The Obama administration created and issued this MyRA account plan in 2015.

As with other types of retirement plans and accounts, participants are able to set up automatic payroll contributions to this account. When they change jobs to work for a different company, the account stays with them as it is their own personal retirement account.

The accounts also provide the distinctive advantage in allowing participants to take out the money they placed in the MyRA account whenever they wish. There is no additional tax levied or penalties assessed at any point when they do this. This means that there is no early withdrawal penalty associated with the MyRA accounts, making it more like a savings account than a government approved retirement plan.

Participants in the MyRA Account like that their money is invested in safe U.S. government Treasuries. The investment is fully backed by the United States Treasury. They state that the account will earn (with no risk) an interest rate of 1.5% APR for the month of July 2016. This is based on the Government Securities Fund. This particular fund earned a 2015 average return of 2.04% and a 2.94% average annual return in the ten year period that concluded in December of 2015.

As a starter retirement account, the MyRA account provides the unmatched benefit of no charges to set up or open it and no ongoing maintenance fees for account owners. It also allows savers to contribute any amount they like with no minimum, even $2 contributions. The investments grow with the same tax advantages as a Roth IRA with after tax dollars. This means that the interest and principle will not be taxable when it is withdrawn from the account at any point between now and through retirement.

The MyRA account does come with maximum contribution limits as do all types of retirement savings vehicles. For tax years 2015 and 2016, participants may contribute no more than $5,500 in the year. If they are older than 49 years of age, this amount increases to $6,500 for the year in catch up contribution amounts which the IRS permits. Besides the annual contribution limit amounts, there are also the same lifetime contribution limits that apply to standard Roth IRA accounts.

Critics of this account have warned that this plan represents an all too easy mark and tempting target for the U.S. government if it runs into financing troubles. In the event that Treasury needs ready to access funds, it would not be able to find any that were easier to seize than the ones it is holding itself on behalf of American account holders. They also accuse the government of setting up a plan that props up and creates demand for Treasuries using Americans' retirement funds as the vehicle to do this.

Options

Options are contracts on stocks, indexes, currencies, commodities, or debt instruments. There are two principle types. These are call options and put options. Call options give holders the ability to purchase a set amount of the underlying instrument for a specific price in a certain amount of time. This specific price is known as the strike price. Put options grant holders the ability to sell the exact amount of the underlying instrument at a fixed price in a given period of time.

With options on stocks, the set amount of the underlying shares that calls and puts cover are typically 100 shares. Option contracts have two parties to them. The first are the sellers who are also known as writers of the option. The buyers are the holders of the option.

Option values are made up of two components. These are intrinsic value and time value. Intrinsic value is the amount that the option is in the money. For an option to be in the money, the stock price must be higher than the strike price for calls. For puts, the stock price has to be lower than the strike price. The value that is left after subtracting intrinsic value is the option's time value. When an option has no intrinsic value, one hundred percent of its value is time value.

Investors can buy and sell options until they run out of time. At this point, they expire either with some intrinsic value or worthless. They can also be exercised. When an option is exercised, the seller must transfer the underlying shares to the holder of the option. When the instrument is not able to be transferred over, then the parties settle in cash instead.

Investors like this financial tool because they give buyers peace of mind. The most an option holder is able to lose is the total price that they paid when they bought the contract. If options are not exercised or sold within the given time frame, then they expire. An option that expires worthless does not involve any exchange of shares or cash.

Buyers and sellers have different potential profits with options. Profit potential is limitless for the buyers. For the sellers, the profit is limited to the price which they receive for the contract. Sellers have unlimited loss potential unless they own the underlying shares or instrument. When a seller of an option holds the underlying instrument, the option is covered.

There are two main reasons that investors buy options. These can be to gain leverage or to obtain protection. The leverage benefit means that the option holder can control a larger amount of equity for a much smaller price than it costs to actually buy the shares. This exposes the buyer to a far smaller potential loss.

Options provide protection to investors who own the shares that underlie the contract. While the owners of the option hold the contract, they gain protection against adverse price movements in their shares. This is because the contract provides the ability to obtain the stock at a certain price during the option's contract time-frame. In this case, the cost of the option is the premium that the owner pays.

There are several downsides to options. The trading costs for options are higher than with buying the underlying shares of the stock or other instrument. This is because the spread between the bid and ask is higher for options. Option commissions also cost more than do stock commissions.

Option trading is more complicated than stock trading too. Options also have to be watched more closely than do stocks generally. The time involved to trade and maintain option strategies can be significant.

Paper Assets

Paper assets have three different meanings depending on whether you are discussing business, investments, or fiat currencies. Where business is concerned, paper assets are assets that you can not easily use or change in to cash. These paper assets possess extremely low liquidity, meaning that they are difficult to sell too. The term in this case literally arises from assets that are valuable on paper, or that have a paper only value.

In investments, paper assets mean something entirely different. They refer to assets that are representations of something. Paper assets in investments literally are pieces of paper that define ownership of an asset. Classic examples of investing paper assets prove to be stocks, currencies, bonds, money market accounts, and similar types of investments. For paper assets to have a tangible value, there must be a working financial system in order to back them up and exchange them. In the cases where a financial system collapses, paper assets commonly sharply decline along with it. The majority of Americans have placed an overwhelming percentage of their money in paper assets, and as the Financial Crisis of 2007-2010 showed, this makes them extremely vulnerable to economic calamities.

Paper assets stand apart in contrast to hard assets. Hard assets contain actual value in the nature of the item itself. There are many forms of hard assets, but among the most popular are gold, silver, diamonds, oil, platinum, land, and other such physical holdings. While financial collapses can cause a set back for the value of hard assets, these types of assets almost always hold up far better than do paper assets.

Many people are shocked by the fact that the U.S. dollar is also a paper asset, as are all Fiat currencies in the world except for the Swiss Franc. These paper currencies are no longer backed up by the long running gold standard. Instead, they only have value because their respective issuing governments, as well as the underlying currency users, say that they do. The Swiss Franc is a lonely exception. The Swiss constitution requires that for every four paper or electronic currency Swiss Francs in existence, there must be one Swiss Franc worth of gold in the Swiss National Bank vaults. Since the Swiss only value their gold holdings at around $250 per ounce, and gold has been trading between $1,300 and $1,400 per ounce for some time now, the Swiss actually have a greater gold backing to their currency than one hundred percent.

Penny Stocks

Penny stocks are those securities that usually trade for comparatively lower prices, off of the big stock exchanges, and with smaller market capitalizations. Many analysts and investors look at these securities as higher in risk and extremely speculative. This is because they feature significant bid and ask spreads, less liquidity, smaller followings, and lesser capitalization and disclosure requirements. Many of these smaller stocks trade on the pink sheets or OTC Bulletin Board in what is known as the "over the counter market."

Penny stocks used to be those which traded for under a dollar, but thanks to the SEC this is no longer the case. The SEC altered the definition so that all stock shares which trade for less than $5 are now considered to be a penny stock. These companies have fewer listing requirements, regulations, and filings which govern them.

It is important to remember that penny stocks best suit investors who can stand more risk. They come with greater amounts of volatility which can lead to steep losses or possibly greater returns. The lower volumes and greater amounts of risk are why the moves in these stocks can be staggering. These companies struggle with fewer resources and less cash, but sometimes achieve breakthroughs that can catapult their share prices higher. It is safer to trade or invest in penny stocks which are listed on the NASDAQ or the AMEX American Stock Exchange because these exchanges more vigorously regulate their constituent companies.

Four factors make these micro cap stocks so much riskier than traditional blue chip stocks. The information which the public has access to is usually lacking. It is harder to make well informed decisions on companies that do not provide sufficient information. Other information that is offered on such micro cap stocks can come from less than reputable sources.

Another feature that makes penny stocks so risky is that they do not have a common set of minimum standards. Neither the pink sheets nor the OTCBB require these companies to live up to minimum requirements to stay listed. They will have to file certain documents in a timely manner with the OTCBB, but not with the pink sheets. These standards traditionally offer a safety cushion that helps to protect investors. They are a benchmark for other smaller companies to achieve.

A third difficulty with these micro cap stocks is they lack history. A great number of such companies could be nearing bankruptcy or recently founded. This means that their track records are either non existent or poor at best. A lack of historical data compounds the difficulty of assessing a company's future and their stock's near and long term possibilities.

A final danger with penny stocks is their lack of liquidity. This creates two problems. An investor may not be able to sell out of the stock at an acceptable price. With low liquidity, there may be no buyer available at any price. Lower liquidity also leads to the possibility for traders to manipulate the prices of the stocks themselves. They can purchase enormous quantities of the issue, promote it themselves, and then sell it at higher prices to other investors who become stuck with it. This is called a pump and dump strategy.

Pivotal Points

Pivotal Points refers to a system for predicting stock price movements that Jesse Livermore created and developed. Time Magazine described him as the most incomparable living American trader of his day. In the 1920's, he used the system to amass a fortune that at its peak valued $100 million. As a share of the U.S. GDP of the time, this amounts to $14 billion in current dollars as measured against today's GDP.

This represented the first time that any investor had documented using Pivotal Points. Livermore famously wrote about it in his book, Reminiscences of a Stock Operator. These Pivotal Points are so useful because more than 90 years after Jesse created them investors still utilize and teach them.

Pivotal Points are the levels at which stock prices find support and resistance. In fact they are the primary levels of both support and resistance, depending on whether they are higher or lower than the price of the stock. Because of the importance of these Pivotal Points, they are the levels where the greatest price movement generally happens. There may be other resistance and support levels. Other levels are less important than the pivotal ones.

There are two principal ways that Pivotal Points are utilized today as they were in the 1920's when Livermore first created them. In the first case, investors can employ them to decide what the general market trend is. Market trend is important because it tells investors which way the market is generally moving.

Should the Pivotal Point price be broken to the upside, then the stock or market proves to be bullish. If instead the Pivotal Point is broken in a downward movement, then an individual investor considers the case to be bearish for the stock or market.

A second way to utilize the Pivotal Points is as a price level for either entering or exiting a trade. Finding the right level to open a position or close out an existing one is critical. Investors can place buy limit orders based on the Pivotal Point resistance level breaking. They might also use the Pivotal Point support level as their stop loss to exit a trade should this critical support line fail.

Nowadays it is easy to figure up Pivotal Points. Computer programs and charting software can find the levels easily. When Jesse first created them, these points had to be manually figured out with no more than a calculator, pencils, and paper. There are a number of formulas that can be used to determine them. Jesse Livermore made his own charts by hand. He looked for the levels where the stocks tended to bounce several times to find them.

Many traders today consider Pivotal Points to be shorter term use indicators. Because a number of investors use them for a single day trading, they have to recalculate them every day. Despite this fact, even day trading Pivotal Points is considered to be helpful. This is because a person can quickly calculate up important levels where there will be significant price movement.

Precious Metals

Precious metals are greatly prized elemental metals. For thousands of years they have been highly valued. These four metals are gold, silver, platinum, and palladium. Most of them have been heavily utilized in jewelry for their resistance to corrosion. Several of these have been used as currency over the centuries.

Today all of them are available as an investment in bullion form. They are widely esteemed as a tangible way to protect the purchasing power of individuals against central banks' unscrupulous money printing activities that debase national currencies. All of the precious metals are rare.

Gold has always been the most readily recognizable of the precious metals. This is because it has a yellow color that is almost unique. The yellow metal has long been beloved for its luster, malleability, and ductile nature. A single ounce of gold can be hammered into sheets that cover 108 square feet (10.03 square meters) and drawn into a thread or wire that stretches 50 miles (80 kilometers). China has become the world's largest gold producer in recent years. Other major producers of it include South Africa, the U.S., and Australia.

For much of the past, only royalty and the very rich could afford to possess gold. From the 1700's until the 1970's, the world's paper money supplies were backed up by gold according to a gold standard that maintained a stable value of money internationally. There has been talk begun by former Federal Reserve Chairman Alan Greenspan of reviving a gold standard in a new international agreement.

Silver is the other ancient member of the precious metals family. It is not only used in coins and jewelry. The grey metal has many uses in industry. This is because it possesses the greatest thermal and electrical conductivity of all elements along with the lowest contact resistance and high reflectivity. This makes it a popular choice in a wide range of electronics, wiring, batteries, antimicrobial demands, dentistry, solar cell panels, RFID devices, and much more. Silver is actually in much higher demand than gold relative to its available supply. Today silver is most heavily produced by Peru, Mexico, China, and Chile.

Silver mining began around 5,000 years ago in modern day Turkey in Anatolia. The Spanish revived its popularity after finding it in the New World. Their mining operations from 1500 to 1800 in Mexico, Peru, and Bolivia amounted to 85% of all global production. It has also served as a standard for paper currencies as the British Empire issued Pound Sterling notes based on the ability to exchange to silver.

Platinum is the rarest of the precious metals on earth. Despite its many industrial uses, it is almost 15 times rarer than gold. Platinum finds use in catalytic converters, weapons, electronics, dentistry, jewelry, and other areas. It has often been more highly priced than gold because of its unique merger of functionality, rarity, and beauty. Platinum is only found in significant quantities in South Africa, Russia, and Canada.

The first people known to mine and work platinum were the South American Indians. They used a smelting process kept secret to the end of the 18th century to produce jewelry and nose rings. Today platinum is sought after in both coin and bullion form by investors and collectors.

Palladium is the least well known of the precious metals group. It is a part of the platinum metals complex. Palladium shares many of platinum's characteristics and properties. It is stable at extreme temperatures, malleable, and rare. Industry uses it for catalytic converters, electronics electrode plating, and to make white gold jewelry. Palladium is produced mostly by Russia, South Africa, Canada, and the U.S. It has become a growing choice as an investible bullion metal as well.

Put Option

Put options are financial contracts that are entered into by two parties, the buyer of the option and the seller, or writer, of the option. They are generally called simply puts. A purchaser is able to establish a long position in a put option by buying the right to actually sell the instrument that underlies the put.

This is done at a particular price called the strike price and is only valid with the options' seller for a certain amount of time. Should you as the buyer of the option choose to exercise your rights, then the seller has to purchase the associated instrument off of you at the price that was set in advance, whatever the present market price proves to be. In consideration for the buyer gaining this option, you pay an option premium amount to the seller of the option.

Put options are a form of insurance against loss. This is because they offer a guaranteed price and purchaser for a given amount of time for an associated instrument. Put option sellers also benefit when they obtain profits for selling you options that you do not choose to exercise. Options are almost never exercised if the instrument's market value stays above the strike price within the put option contract time frame.

You as a buyer of a put option also have the ability to make money. This is done by selling the associated instrument for a higher price and buying back the position for a significantly lower market price. When an option is not sold or exercised, it expires worthless, representing a total loss of the premium paid for it.

When you purchase a put, you do so with the idea that the associated asset price will decline by the expiration date. The other reason for taking on such a put option is to safe guard a position that you own in the asset or security. Purchasing a put option provides an advantage as compared to selling a stock short. The most that you can lose with a put option is the money that you have paid for it, while those who sell short have an unlimited loss potential. The downside to a put is that the gain potential is restricted to a certain amount. This turns out to be the strike price of the option minus the spot price of the associated asset and the premium that you pay for the option.

A seller or writer of a put feels confident that the associated asset price will go up or remain the same but not decline. Sellers of puts engage in this activity in order to collect premiums. A writer of a put has a limited loss equal to the strike price of the put minus the spot price and the premium that has already been obtained. Put options can similarly be utilized to reduce a risk in the option seller's investment portfolio. They can be part of complicated strategies called option spreads.

A put option that is not covered by owning the underlying security or asset is referred to as a naked put. In these types of put scenarios, the investor might hope to build up a position in the stock that underlies the options so long as they can get a cheap enough price. If you the buyer do not exercise these options, then the seller of the put gets to keep the premium that you paid for the option, representing a profit to the seller.

Should the associated stock's actual price be lower than the strike price of the option when the expiration date comes, then you as a buyer have the ability to exercise the put option in question. This makes the seller of the put option purchase the associated stock at the strike price of the option. You as a buyer would profit to the amount of the difference found between the market price of the stock and the strike price of the option. Yet, should the price of the stock prove to be higher than the strike price of the option on the expiration day, this option becomes worthless. The loss to the owner of the option is restricted to the money that you paid for it, which then becomes the profit to the put option seller.

Residual

Residual refers to residual income. Residual income can have several different meanings depending on the context that you use. For an individual, residual income proves to be the money that remains at the end of a month after all financial responsibilities for the month are covered.

These include living costs, taxes, and housing costs. Where business is concerned, residual incomes are the operating income that is additional as compared to the typical minimum amount of operating assets that are controlled. Residual income furthermore refers to passive income that is earned. In this form of the term, it relates to all income that is created as a result of activities that are indirect. These might include royalties, rental income, investment portfolio returns, website revenues, or passively managed businesses, all of which qualify as residual income.

The word residual is a variation on the word residue. Residue means anything that stays behind because of some other substance or cause. So, residual income proves to be additional money made because of another activity like penning a novel and collecting royalties for the sale of every book.

Rental incomes are residual as they remain from the action of buying a house and then renting it to a tenant who pays you a monthly rental fee. Work is involved in this activity, although a property management company can do it on your behalf. The rewards for this rental project can be significant, as you enjoy the continuous rental stream as well as any increases in the value of the real estate property underlying it. Rental income can be utilized to pay for potentially an entire mortgage.

Income from investment portfolios is similarly considered to be residual income. Both dividends and interest are acquired as an additional, passive benefit of possessing stocks, bonds, mutual funds, and other instruments. This residual income is not guaranteed from these investments, but it is common for investors.

A form of residual income that is growing in popularity these days is website, or Internet based, revenues. Internet revenues are commonly those that you make from having advertising on a given website. The dollar value of the advertising is mostly based on the number of visitors to the page. A significant amount of start up work is required to create the website and get it highly ranked on the major search engines. After this, you can see continuous monthly profits that you earn as a result of the advertising, which builds up a residual income. This amount of money could be as little as a few dollars a month to possibly thousands of dollars per month.

A last form of residual income can result from a business. If your company becomes large enough, you may be able to hire a manager to run it. The income that supports you while the manager runs the business is then considered residual income.

Reverse Split

A reverse split is also known as a reverse stock split. Reverse splits are used to reduce the total outstanding number of a given company's shares. This action boosts the value of its stock and the resulting earnings per share. Not everything concerning a stock changes in a reverse stock split. One thing that remains the same is the market capitalization. Market capitalization refers to the value price of the total outstanding number of shares.

A reverse split works by a certain process. In this scenario, a company involved will actually cancel out the presently existing shares for every share holder. They will replace these with a smaller number of new shares. These new shares will be issued in an exact proportion to your original stake in the company.

Such a reverse split proves to be the exact opposite of a stock split. Reverse splits can also be called stock merges, since they literally reduce the total number of outstanding shares and proportionally increase the price per share. Companies commonly issue the reverse split shares according to an easy to understand ratio. You might receive one new share for every two old shares, or possibly four new shares for every old five ones that you owned.

Looking at an example of the way that a reverse stock split actually works is helpful. Say that a company in which you own stock shares decided to affect a one for ten reverse split. If you had one thousand shares of the company, then you would only own one hundred shares of the resulting issue. This would not change the value of the shares that you held though, as the price of the shares would increase by ten times. If the shares had been worth only four dollars per share, now they would be valued at forty dollars per share.

There are several reasons why companies choose to do a reverse split of their stock shares. They might feel that the actual price per share of their stock is so low that it is not appealing to new investors. Some institutions are only allowed to buy shares that trade at a certain minimum value, such as five dollars per share or higher. Reverse stock splits can also be used to reduce the number of share holders, since they can force smaller shareholders to be cashed out, which means that they no longer possess any shares of the company. In this case, you would receive the value of your shares in cash.

There is a negative connotation associated with engaging in reverse stock splits. Because of this reason, they are not done lightly by companies. A company might find that its share price has declined so precipitously that it becomes in danger of having its shares de-listed from the stock exchange. They could quickly boost the share price with the reverse split. Stocks that have undergone a reverse split will usually have the letter D added to the end of their symbol tickers.

A board of directors for a given company is allowed to perform a reverse split without consulting with its share holders to obtain their approval. The Securities and Exchange Commission also does not have any say over such reverse stock splits. They are instead regulated by a state's corporate laws and the company's own articles of incorporation, along with the company's by laws.

Risk Averse

Risk averse investors are those who fear or are intolerant of risk. Given a chance to pick from two investments with similar returns they will go with the one that offers the lesser risk. This is because risk averse investors do not like risk.

Because of this they will avoid investing in stocks and other investments that they consider to be higher risk. This means that they will likely miss out on greater rates of return as a result of their more cautious investing approach. These investors who look out for investments they perceive to be safer will tend to go with government bonds and index funds. Both of these typically offer lower returns.

Studies have been done that show investors will tend to avoid risk that is unnecessary. This is a subjective measurement because every investor has a varying definition of what is unnecessary risk. Those investors who wish to obtain a greater return will understand that a larger amount of risk is necessary. Individuals who are satisfied with a lower return would consider this type of investment strategy foolhardy. The overwhelming majority of economic players are risk averse enough to choose an investment that is less risky if it offers the same return as a riskier investment.

Risk averse markets are those which are afraid of geopolitical or economic events. When the markets are like this they favor safer havens such as gold and the precious metals, Swiss Francs, Treasury bonds, and U.S. dollars. In risk averse markets, investors tend to shun higher risk stocks and securities and try to preserve their investment capital from losses. The opposite of these are risk tolerant markets.

Risk aversion is the representation of individual's and investor's all around preference to have certainty over uncertainty. Because of this, they attempt to reduce the repercussions of the worst potential outcomes that lie before them. Risk aversion means that people will prefer to stay in a low paying job that offers perceived job security rather than to become an entrepreneur who has the chance to make a great amount of money as well as to lose all of the money and time that is invested.

Risk aversion will drive these individuals to seek out a lower rate of return with their investment and savings capital. They would rather have a savings account or certificate of deposit than equities. Even though equities offer much greater potential returns than these other instruments, they are far riskier and can deliver negative returns. A great number of risk averse investors will give extreme weight to the worst possible scenario. It does not matter that the probabilities of these occurring are low. They will shy away from these investments because losses could happen.

Studies have determined that risk aversion comes from an individual's experience. This is particularly true of the economic situation they experienced while a child. Those who grew up in harder economic times are more likely to handle and invest their money far differently from those who grew up in prosperous times.

A classic example concerns Americans who grew up in the 1930's Great Depression. This group has always tended to be extremely risk averse about career or job changes. They are typically extremely conservative with their money. They also avoid the stock market as much as possible as they remember the Black Thursday and Black Monday crashes of 1929.

Financial advisers and planners must understand the risk tolerance and aversion of their clients clearly. They can not recommend the appropriate investments and risk level without this. They will invest the money of a risk averse individual far differently than that of a person who is risk tolerant.

Risk Premium

A risk premium turns out to be the surplus return over the risk free rate of return which investments are anticipated to provide. Any asset offers such a premium as a means of rewarding those investors who are willing to take on the additional risk as opposed to an asset which is risk free. Examples of this abound.

Excellent credit rated companies' corporate bonds do not entail much, if any, risk of default. This is because such businesses have a proven track record of paying their debts in a timely fashion and significant profits as well as cash flow. It is ultimately why these types of bonds deliver a substantially lower yield or interest payment than do bonds from companies which are less well established and have uncertain financials leading to a greater risk of default.

Risk premium could be regarded as a form of hazard pay for investment portfolios. This is much like those employees who perform jobs deemed to be dangerous and obtain a hazard pay in compensation for the risks in which they engage on the job. Similarly, risky types of investments have to offer investors the possibility of greater returns in order to justify the higher risks which the investment involves.

Investors only undertake such perilous investments because they anticipate receiving appropriate compensation for the level of risk they assume. They receive this in the form of a risk premium, or higher returns above the rates of return that such low risk investments as U.S. Treasury issued securities provide. Another way of putting it is that because investors might lose money thanks to the insecurity of a given investment, they receive higher returns as their reward should the investment work out successfully. The possibility of obtaining such a premium does not guarantee that investors will actually receive it. This is because the borrower could go bankrupt or default if the outcome of the investment is not at least partially successful.

Such a risk premium may be a gratifying recompense because investments which are riskier are naturally more profitable if and when they turn out to be successful. Those investments which possess predictable and sure outcomes will not evolve into financial breakthroughs as they are already successfully performing in markets that are well developed. This is why risky and creative investment and business initiatives are the ones which could possibly provide returns that are better than average. The borrowing entity rewards its investors for taking on their risk in backing the idea or business effort. Because of this fact, some investors have been willing to seek out and fund riskier investments with the hope of obtaining significantly greater payouts.

The truth is that such a risk premium is expensive for the companies who borrow. This is more the case if their various investments or ideas will not necessarily pan out as the most successful or lucrative ones. The greater the premium these companies promise their investors as compensation for the entailed risk, the higher a financial burden they experience. Such burdens can actually be detrimental to the success of their endeavors and lead to greater chance of a final default.

This is why investors' best interest lies in tempering the amount of risk premium they insist on from their investments. The alternative is that they will have to line up and battle against other debt collectors if the company they backed financially defaults in the end. The sad truth is that with many bankruptcies heavily mired in debt, most investors recover only a matter of cents on their dollars, regardless of how high the risk premium offered initially proved to be.

Rollover IRA

An IRA is the acronym for Individual Retirement Account. These accounts represent a form of government-approved and -created savings account for retirement. They have several advantages, the main one of which is the significant tax breaks they receive in tax deferment. This makes them the optimal way to put cash aside towards eventual retirement. It is important to know that IRAs are not investments. Instead they are more like the basket in which individuals maintain their mutual funds, stocks, bonds, and other assets. When one retirement account is transferred to another one, this is known as a Rollover IRA.

Generally people open such a Rollover IRA themselves. There are also a few types which small business owners and the self employed can open. Among the various types of Individual Retirement Accounts in existence are the Roth IRAs, traditional IRAs, SEP IRAs, and SIMPLE IRAs. Not all of these can be accessed by every individual in the U.S. This is to say that every one of them has specific eligibility requirements which revolve around the type of employment and income level. What they do all have in common is the caps on the amount individuals are allowed to contribute every year. They also mostly share steep penalties for withdrawing funds ahead of the government set age of retirement.

The greatest benefit to these accounts lies in their ability for all of the assets within the plan to gain in value while not being taxed by the U.S. Federal government. This means that all income generated by capital gains, dividends, and interest will compound every year with no tax bite. Taxes on the majority of these forms of IRAs only become due as the owners take qualified (or unqualified with a penalty) distributions. There are two different forms of this. With the majority of the IRAs, individuals are able to commit pre-taxed dollars to the account. With Roth IRAs, the dollars are after-taxed, but then no additional taxes on them will be required upon withdrawals at retirement. Using the Rollover IRA concept, individuals can switch from one type of IRA to another.

The Internal Revenue Service strictly limits how much money people can put into such accounts. The majority of individuals who are less than 50 are not permitted to contribute over $5,500 each year as of 2016. These limits become higher once the holders attain an age greater than 50. They call this "catch up contributions," and the limits are typically raised by $1,000 to $1,500 more in this decade immediately before holders reach retirement age.

Practically all individuals are allowed to make contributions each year to a traditional form of IRA. So long as either the holder or spouse earns taxable income and is less than 70 and a half years old, they can participate.

The various kinds of IRAs are important to understand. A ROTH IRA does not provide tax deductions on contributions. There are also income restrictions which in 2016 amounted to under $184,000 for married filing jointly families or $117,000 for single heads of households or those who are married filing separately and not living with their spouses.

Both SEP and SIMPLE IRAs apply to only small business owners and the self employed. Only employers who claim fewer than 100 employees can set up these SIMPLE IRA accounts. Any individual who possesses freelancing income or who owns a business can open an SEP IRA.

While individuals can always withdraw their contributions (and even earnings) at any point once they have deposited them to their IRAs, there are penalties if they are less than 59 and ½ years old. The penalty is an extra 10 percent above the that-year tax bracket of the individuals who take distributions early. The government's point is to discourage people from utilizing their retirement accounts like ATM machines or credit cards.

Roth IRA

A Roth IRA is a particular type of Individual Retirement Account. These Roth IRA's prove to be special retirement plans that are given favorable tax treatment. The tax laws of the United States permit tax reductions on restricted amount savings for retirement accounts.

Roth IRA's are different from other IRA's in several ways. Among the chief of these is that tax breaks are not given on monies that are put into the plan and account with a Roth IRA. Instead, these tax breaks are given out on the money and its investment gains when they are taken out of the account at retirement. This chief appeal of Roth IRA's is that they provide completely tax free income at retirement.

Other Roth IRA benefits over traditional forms of IRA's exist as well. The restrictions placed on the kinds of investments that they are allowed to contain are fewer. You can turn them into gold IRA's and annuity account IRA's. Roth IRA's can also contain all of the usual forms of investments that IRA's contain, such as mutual funds, stocks, bonds, and certificates of deposit. More unusual investments such as real estate, mortgage notes, derivatives, and even franchises are allowed to be purchased with Roth IRA's. These investment choices do depend on the capability and allowance of the Roth IRA trustee, or firm with which the plan is set up. Roth IRA's also permit you to make un-penalized withdrawals of all direct contributions that you make, after the first five years of the account have and plan have passed, which is certainly not the case with traditional IRA's.

These distributions, or withdrawals, are not taxed because they are taxed before the contributions are made. The penalties are waived for principal, as well as interest and earnings in the account, if the distributions are for purchasing a house or for disability or retirement withdrawal uses. If there is not a justified reason for the distribution, then the account earnings and income made above contributions will be taxed.

All IRA's contain specific limits on the dollar amount of contributions that the government permits. This amount changes per year, and is set through the year 2011 now. Presently, you can put $5,000 per year into Roth IRA's. There are income restrictions that govern whether you are allowed to make this full contribution as well. Individuals who make less than $106,000 are permitted to make full Roth IRA contributions, and those who make under $121,000 may make a partial contribution. Married couples who file together are allowed to earn less than $167,000 to make their full contribution to the Roth IRA, while those who make under $177,000 can do a partial contribution.

Roth IRA conversions from traditional IRA's have been allowed by the IRA in the past, although with certain income restrictions. Beginning in 2010, this policy changed. Now the IRS permits any persons, regardless of how much money that they make, to convert their traditional IRA's into Roth IRA's.

SDR Denominated Bonds

SDR denominated bonds are a fairly recent phenomenon. These are bonds issued in special drawing rights currency units. SDR units are a basket of the world's most important currencies including the U.S. dollar, Euro zone euro, Japanese Yen, British pound sterling, and the Chinese Yuan. The International Monetary Fund's executive board approved a framework to issue such bonds to member nations and central banks back on July 1, 2009.

The principle of these SDR denominated bonds was intended to be allocated in SDRs. The market for such bonds was established initially as the official sector of IMF members. This meant it was to include primarily the member nations, relevant central banks, and another 15 holders of SDRs.

Included in these 15 prescribed holders are four central banks which were regional, eight developmental organizations, and three monetary agencies which were intergovernmental. Others allowed to trade in them were the fiscal agencies of the members. This means that a number of sovereign wealth funds were allowed to participate as there are not always distinguishing lines between national monetary authorities and their sovereign wealth funds. This is the case with Hong Kong and Saudi Arabia.

The IMF issued SDR denominated bonds were to start with three month maturities that could be extended to as long as five years. Interest payments on these instruments were quarterly. China signed an agreement to buy upwards of $50 billion of them, while Russia, India, and Brazil intended to buy as much as $10 billion each.

SDR denominated bonds again gained the international spotlight in August of 2016 when the World Bank's IBRD International Bank for Reconstruction and Development priced the first such bond in the Interbank Bond Market of China. This bond raised 500 million SDR units, which were equal to about $700 million US dollars. These bonds came with a three year maturity date. Their coupon interest payment rate was .49% per year. What made them most notable was that the payments are issued in Chinese Yuan.

This group of bonds is only the first batch. The full size of the issue approved by the World Bank SDR Denominated Issuance Program in August 12, 2016 is for 2 billion SDR's, making them equal to roughly $2.8 billion US dollars.

Even in China, placing so many SDR denominated bonds is a challenge. This is why the joint lead managers for the Interbank Market were several important banks with great depth in China. These included HSBC Bank of China Company Limited, the Commercial Bank of China Limited, China Development Bank Corporation, and China Construction Bank Corporation.

The issue was a great success. The significant interest in them led to a 2.5 times oversubscribing. Orders amounted to roughly 50. Fifty-three percent of them came from bank treasuries, 29 percent from central banks and official institutions, 12 percent from asset managers and securities firms, and six percent from insurance companies. These bonds will mature on September 2, 2019 with all payments coming from the World Bank's IBDR to be made to bond holders in Chinese Yuan.

Selling Short

Selling short, or short selling, is a strategy used in trading stocks. In the selling short process, you borrow the shares of the stock in question from your stock broker. You then turn around and sell the stock shares borrowed for a certain price that the market offers. Your hope is that the price of the stock will drop, so that you can buy back the stock shares for a lesser amount. This creates a profit for your transaction. The practice is buying low and selling high done in the reverse order.

If the price of the stock drops, then this process of short selling makes you money. The down side to it is that when the price of the stock instead rises, then you lose money. Detractors of selling short claim that you can subject yourself to an unlimited amount of risk, since stock prices could rise without stopping. This means that you could potentially lose more than the amount of money that you invest if a given stock that you sold short took off and ran away without you closing out the transaction. Profits are limited by the distance of the stock price to zero, since a share's price can never decline below zero.

Such selling short trades are closed out by repurchasing the shares that you sold short earlier. When it is time to close out the transaction by buying back the shares, this is called covering. The other names for this process are buy to cover or simply cover.

There are risks involved in selling short stocks. The biggest risk is that the stock could go up indefinitely. For example, you might sell short ten shares of IBM's stock at $100 per share. This means that you have put a thousand dollars into the trade. If the stock later declined to ninety, then you would realize a gain of one hundred dollars. If instead it rose to $130 before you covered it, then you would lose three hundred dollars. While the lowest that the IBM shares might decline is to zero, potentially making you as much as one thousand dollars in profits, they could also rise to three hundred dollars, losing you two thousand dollars.

Short sellers can also fall victim to a short squeeze. As the stock price that you have shorted rises, some investors who shorted it will choose to limit their losses by buying the stock back. Still other investors may have no choice but to buy back the shares in order to satisfy any margin calls on their declining valued position. All of this buying back to cover creates a bigger increase in the price of the stock. The final outcome is a large move up in the price of the stock that creates significant losses for those who continue to be short the stock.

Share Repurchase

Share Repurchase refers to a company program where the corporation purchases back some of its own shares off of the stock markets or from its own individual investors. There are various reasons why a company would choose to spend its excess profits or cash reserves on such an activity. Generally management believes the price of the stock is unfairly undervalued. This repurchase activity allows them to decrease the total number of shares which are outstanding while making a vote of confidence in the company's prospects.

The company can go about this in one or more of several ways. They might purchase shares directly from the stock market. They could also provide their existing shareholders with the opportunity of selling their shares back to the firm at a set and agreed upon price.

Companies would be interested in decreasing the quantity of shares which are outstanding on the markets as this directly boosts the earnings per share when they retire the shares which they have repurchased. Shares that they buy back they either cancel out or keep as treasury stock. In either case, they are no longer held by investors or traded publically.

This kind of share repurchase does a number of beneficial things for the financial balance sheets of the firms which engage in them. Since it decreases the aggregate assets of the business in question, this means that the firm's return on equity, return on assets, and various other measurements of corporate health all improve. The earnings per share (EPS), cash flow, and total revenues also increase faster with fewer outstanding shares. When the business decides to still pay out the identical sum of cash in dividends to its shareholders each year, and the full number of existing shares decreases, then each shareholder will receive a bigger yearly dividend amount.

When the corporation in question increases both its earnings per share and accompanying all around dividends declaration, then reducing the outstanding numbers of shares will boost the dividend growth rate as well. Stock holders are demanding by nature and will expect their company to continue to pay out consistent and growing dividends year in and year out. These share repurchase actions reduce the amount of reserve capital which the business must keep on hand to match the par value of outstanding shares so that they could return a greater amount of capital back to shareholders when they decrease the outstanding amounts of shares.

It is easier to visualize this with a tangible real world example. A company may wish to give out 75 percent of the total earnings to the stake holders and still maintain a consistent dividend payout ratio of 50 percent. The other 25 percent of earnings they could distribute by engaging in a share repurchase program via buying back shares as a complement to the dividend.

Companies buy back their shares because they are convinced that their stock price is significantly undervalued. They believe that this is an efficient means of sinking company money into a vehicle which is also putting the money back into the pockets of shareholders. Each share gains a larger percentage ownership of the company as a result of this endeavor, increasing the value and percentage of each stakeholder's position in the corporation. Such a share repurchase program will also convince potentially skeptical investors that the business maintains more than sufficient minimum capital reserves for difficult economic cycles and corporate emergencies.

A possible downside to such share repurchase plans lies in the impression that they can convey to analysts and investors alike. It might give out the possibly erroneous idea that the firm has no better prospects in which to sink its excess funds. This could mean that they recognize no good potential opportunities to grow the business. For those investors seeking both revenue and turnover increases, this is the wrong message to send. It is also true that spending the company rainy day fund to buy back shares will prove to be a terrible idea if there is a dramatic downturn in the economy afterwards.

Stock Buybacks

Stock buybacks occur when companies repurchase their own company shares from the markets. They are sometimes called share repurchases. A buyback is like a company choosing to invest in itself, since it is actually employing its own cash reserve to purchase its own stock.

Companies may not be shareholders in themselves, which means that their shares are absorbed back into the company. This has a net effect of decreasing the quantities of stock share which are outstanding. This also increases the size of each owner's stake in the company as there are not as many shares and claims on the company's earnings.

There are two means in which stock buybacks occur. They can be done via tender offers or open market purchases. In a tender offer, all shareholders receive such a tender offer from the company to submit some or all of their shares by a specific deadline. Such an offer divulges the quantities of shares which the company wishes to buy back as well as the price range they are agreeable to offer.

These tenders are nearly always at premium prices versus the current market level. Investors who are interested in participating will let the company know how many shares they wish to sell them at the price they will take. The company involved in the share repurchase would then put together the right combinations so that it could purchase the shares it wants for the lowest price.

Companies can also enter the open markets to engage in stock buybacks. They do this precisely as individual investors by buying shares at the going market price. The difference between the company and an individual investor doing this is that the market sees a company repurchasing its own shares as a significantly positive action. This generally leads to the stock prices rising quickly.

A company management will state that the share repurchase is their best option for deploying the firm's excess capital at that given point in time. The management of a firm is supposed to be interested in maximizing the returns for their stake holders. These stock buybacks do usually boost the value of shareholders. There are other motives for company managements buying back shares. They may believe that the stock market has overly discounted the prices of its stock shares.

Stock prices can decline from many different causes. These might be that earnings were less than anticipated, the economy is poor, or there are negative rumors surrounding the company. Firms that pay out millions of dollars to invest in their own shares show that the company management feels the market has punished their share prices unfairly with the discount. This is always seen positively.

Stock buybacks can also create better fundamentals for a company's balance sheet. Since the repurchased shares become either cancelled or treasury stock, this lowers the number of outstanding shares as a result. This decreases the balance sheet assets as the cash is spent. With fewer assets on the balance sheet, the return on assets ROA goes up in the process. Return on equity ROE also grows as the outstanding equity is reduced. The markets generally prefer higher ROAs and ROEs. Managements that do share buybacks just to boost their balance sheet fundamentals are looked at negatively and as problematic.

Stock Split

Stock splits occur when corporations decide to expand the number of underlying shares in the company. They do this by setting out a ratio for the stock split. They might say that for every one share of stock, there will now be two, which would double your existing shares. This would be called a two to one stock split.

If you had one hundred shares of the stock before the split that were trading at twenty dollars per share, then you would possess fifty shares of the stock trading at ten dollars each share after the split occurred. The value of the total shares owned does not change as a result of a stock split, only the amounts of shares that you possess and the per share price of the stock in question. In either case, they would still be worth two thousand dollars.

Companies mostly engage in stock splits because of a liquidity motivation. There are many companies that feel that more expensive stocks keep investors from buying them. By splitting the shares, the price of the shares declines proportionally. They hope that this will result in a scenario where greater quantities of shares of the stock are then purchased and sold. The downside to this argument is that the higher volume of the shares traded could cause larger drops and increases in the price of the stock, which leads to greater volatility in the share prices.

While numerous investors believe that stock splits are beneficial, there is no real evidence to support this feeling. Stocks do not automatically rise back to the price that they maintained in advance of the split. The extra shares do not result in greater amounts of dividends being realized by the investors either, since each share then represents proportionally smaller earnings, assets, and dividends of the company involved in the split.

While most companies go through stock splits as the price rises, a select few have steadfastly refused to do so. Berkshire Hathaway proves to be the most famous case of this. In the 1960's, it traded at only $8 each share. In recent decades, you have seen its value jump up to $150,000 per share. The Washington Post has also seen its non splitting shares trade upwards of six hundred dollars each. The shareholder base of both companies has remained consistent and stable as a result of not splitting the stock shares.

Tax-Deferred

Tax deferred money and status pertains to earnings on investments. This includes dividends, interest, and capital gains which are allowed to accumulate without taxes paid until the owner withdraws the earnings and gains. The two most popular kinds of these deferred investments are found in IRAs and tax deferred annuities. Growth that is tax deferred permits gains to be compounded instead of having taxes paid on them.

Investors gain in two different ways from having taxes deferred on their investment returns. The first method is through growth on investments which is tax free. Instead of having to pay taxes on the present returns of the investment, the taxes are not paid until a later time. This allows the investment to increase without setbacks.

The second method from tax deferral pertains to investments which are entered in pre-retirement accumulation phases. At this point, the earnings and taxes on them are generally significantly higher than earnings will be when the owners retire. This means that withdrawals drawn out of deferred accounts typically happen after individuals are bringing in less taxable income. The end result is that their tax rate is at a lower level than the one the IRS applies with they are still working.

There are a number of qualified and approved tax deferred vehicles available today. Probably the most common and popular is the 401(k). Employers provide these plans as a company benefit to help their employees to increase their retirement savings.

Third party administrators act to deduct contributions from employee payrolls and help manage the plans. The employees then get to choose from several options in which to invest their tax deferred savings. These include company stock, mutual funds, or some fixed rate choices. All gains made in these accounts do no add to the taxable earnings of the employees participating. These contributions they make to the 401(k) and other qualified accounts like most IRAs come from pre-taxed dollars. This means that the employee's taxable income amount becomes reduced.

When the employees surpass the minimum 59.5 retirement age, they are able to take distributions from these plans. The taxes they pay are only those which apply on their earnings as they are received. So investors who may earn enough to pay 33% tax bracket while employed will likely pay as little as 10% to 15% taxes on distributions they take from their 401(k) plans at retirement that they have along with their any other income from interest, social security, or pensions.

401(k)s typically involved employer dollar matching programs that inspire employees to set aside a greater amount of their earnings in order to increase the size of their retirement nest egg. In putting the money off to the future, they will pay fewer taxes in the end.

It is important to understand the difference between tax deferred and non tax deferred retirement vehicles. Some retirement investment accounts are not tax deferred. The owners pay the taxes on the earnings before they contribute them to the accounts. The advantage to this is that all interest, dividends, and capital gains grow without any other taxes being owed on them when they are taken out as distributions at retirement age. One beloved insurance product that works this way is an annuity.

Retirement plans like traditional IRAs have annual contribution limits of $5,500 per year as of 2016. Annuities do not come with such annual restriction levels. Employees can contribute even millions of dollars per year to them if they wish.

The earnings made in these insurance backed products grow without having taxes taken out of them even at retirement. This means that any and all earnings in these account compound fully from the second year of the annuity contract. So long as the gains earned are taken out after the employee reaches 59.5, there will not be any taxes or early withdrawal penalties of 10% levied against the earnings in these pre-taxed contribution accounts.

Tenure Annuity

A Tenure Annuity is a type of reverse mortgage monthly payment plan. This program delivers cash payments that are consistent to the home owning seniors for an unlimited amount of time until they pass away or move out of the house. The agreement remains in force up to the point that both spouses leave the house that backs the loan. Tenure payment amounts are usually fixed based on the primary borrower's age.

Such a tenure annuity can be crucial for those seniors who do not have much monthly income or savings. They likely still want to take advantage of activities which provide an active and enjoyable retirement. The monthly payments from these tenure annuities can be used at the discretion of the borrower. They might use them to supplement benefits from social security. Medical costs can be paid with them. Seniors can work to pay down debts using the funds or to improve, renovate, or repair their home. They can even put them to use for leisure activities and travel opportunities.

Financial planners often advise seniors to increase their retirement income streams using a tenure annuity. This is because the income from private pensions and/or social security is often insufficient to meet their expenses and desires. There are many benefits to these plans. One of the most important is that they deliver a guaranteed and predictable monthly payment that boosts other income sources.

A tenure annuity has numerous other advantages. The money will be provided for as long as the borrowers live in the house, whether this is for from a few months to several decades. The arrangement is fully covered and backed by the FHA Federal Housing Administration. The borrowers continue to enjoy complete and unrestricted use of their house that is tied to the reverse mortgage. There is no burden of monthly mortgage payments as with a traditional mortgage loan. Finally, there are no additional collateral requirements besides the house itself.

One of the valuable characteristics of a tenure annuity is that the debt builds up against the home slowly. The equity for the future payments remains in the house until it is needed. This means that the estate of the borrowers will be significantly greater if they die early than for a senior who simply took out the maximum cash value in the reverse mortgage.

A tenure annuity also provides flexibility for the senior borrower. These participants are able to modify the transaction by simply paying a minor $20 fee to the loan servicer.

As an example, a borrower who determines he or she will not require the monthly tenure payment amount for some time can change the house's unused equity over to a credit line. The credit line increases in size every month as the payment amounts of the annuity build up in the line. In a case where the opposite is true, seniors who require bigger payment amounts are able to switch over into the term annuity from the line of credit.

Another useful feature of the tenure annuities is that they protect the value of the property from declining. Whether the borrower chooses the monthly payments, the credit line, or switches back and forth, the protection remains the same. Thanks to the FHA coverage of the reverse mortgage, the borrower is not liable for any declines in the value of the home.

Treasury Bonds

Treasury Bonds are also called T-Bonds. These financial instruments prove to be government debt issued by the United States federal government at a fixed rate of interest. Such debt securities come with maturity dates of longer than 10 years. The T-bonds offer interest payments twice per year. Because they are federal debt instruments, their earned income may only be taxed by the federal level authorities of the Internal Revenue Service. Though nothing is really risk free in the investing world, investors generally consider these bonds to be virtually without risk, since they are issued by the United States federal government. Investors perceive them to have a minimal amount of default risk.

Such Treasury Bonds turn out to be among the four kinds of Department of Treasury issued debt. They employ all of these to finance the runaway spending activities of the Federal Government. In these four debt types are the T-bills, Treasury notes, T-bonds, and TIPS Treasury Inflation Protected Securities. Each of these different debt securities is different according to both their coupon payments and their varying maturities.

Despite this, every one of them are the benchmarks for their particular fixed income categories. This is because they are American government backed, almost free of risk, and guaranteed by the revenues and tax base of the United States Treasury. In theory the Treasury can always levy higher taxes to make sure the interest and principles are repaid on these financial instruments. As they are all the lowest returns in their investment category, they are also deemed to be benchmarks for the various fixed income types of investments.

Such Treasury Bonds come standard issued with maturities which vary from 10 years to as long as 30 years. Their denominations start at $1,000 minimums. Each coupon interest payment pays out on a semi-annual basis. The bonds themselves sell via an auction system. The most of them that investors can purchase is $5 million when the bid proves to be non-competitive or as much as a full 35 percent of the entire issues when the bids turn out to be competitive.

It is important to understand what a competitive bid actually is. These types of bids declare that the bidder will accept a certain minimum interest rate bid. These become accepted according to the comparison versus the bond's set rate. With noncompetitive bids, bidders are guaranteed to receive the bonds so long as they will take them at the pre-set interest rate. Once the bonds have been auctioned off, the buyers may sell them off via the secondary market.

Investors call the active market for Treasury bonds re-sales the secondary market. Thanks to this enormous market, T-bonds and T-bills are extremely liquid. It means they can be easily resold on a constant continuous basis. It is this secondary market that causes the T-bonds' prices to gyrate considerably in the markets. This is why both yield rates and current auction rates for the T-bonds determine their prices via the secondary market.

As with all other kinds of standard bonds, these Treasury bonds will experience declining prices as the rates at auction increase. Conversely, the bonds will experience rising prices when the auction rates decrease. The reason for this inverse relationship is that the future cash flows of such bonds becomes discounted according to the higher rate.

T-bonds are also important because they are part of the yield curve for the fixed income markets. As one of the four principal investments which the American federal government offers, they make up this yield curve. The curve is critical because it pictorially displays the range of maturity yields. It is typically sloping upward since lower maturities provide lower rates than do the farther out maturity varieties. There are cases though when the farther out maturities experience peak demand. This causes the yield curve to become inverted. In such a scenario, the farther out maturities will have lower rates than the closer dated maturities.

1035 Exchange

A 1035 Exchange is an exchange process that permits individuals to replace their existing life insurance policy or annuity contract with a similar new contract or policy. Thanks to a provision in the tax code, this can be affected without suffering any negative tax repercussions as part of the trade off exchange. The Internal Revenue Service permits those who hold these kinds of contracts to update their old policies and annuities with those more modern ones that include better benefits, superior investment choices, and lower fees.

The 1035 Exchange is also called a Section 1035 Exchange after the tax code section for which it is named. It literally permits policyholders to transfer their funds out of an endowment, life insurance policy, or annuity into a newer similar vehicle. The way it works is to allow holders to defer their gains. When all of the received proceeds of the original contract become transferred to the newer contract (as there are simultaneously not any loans outstanding on the prior policy), no tax becomes due at point of exchange. Should these proceeds be received and not exchanged according to the 1035 Exchange rules, then all gains obtained out of the first contract become taxable like ordinary income, and not as capital gains.

Gains do not refer to all money received. Instead they are the result of subtracting the gross cash value from the premium tax basis. This basis refers to the original dollar amount put into the contract itself minus the premiums paid for extra benefits or any distributions which qualify as tax free.

In order for this 1035 Exchange to make sense, it has to benefit the policy holder either economically or personally. It is also important for holders to never terminate their in place insurance policies until the newer policy has been fully issued and becomes effective. The holders need to contemplate any health changes since the original policy started. It might cost extra premiums in order for the newer policy to cover them. They might even receive a denial of coverage if the changes in health are too drastic. Similarly, if the holder is well advanced in age, the premium rate may increase.

Some policies also have surrender charges that must be considered. There may be different guarantees, provisions, and interest crediting in the newer policy as well. Most importantly, benefits of the newer policy have to be carefully reviewed. These may change negatively in some cases.

There are rare cases where simply surrendering an existing insurance policy or annuity is more advantageous than engaging in a 1035 Exchange. These primarily occur when the existing contract offers no gain. Sometimes outstanding loans on the initial policy also decrease the benefits of an exchange. In other cases, the original policy may have a "market rate adjustment" type of provision. This would cause the exchange proceeds to be less than those offered in a surrender.

It is usually the case that such a 1035 Exchange will be slower and more involved than simply surrendering the holder's original policy. It can even require a few months much of the time. This is why the conditions that affect the practicality of the exchange include financial conditions of the initial policy carrier, the country's economic climate at the time, and the intentions of the policy holder.

The IRS only deems certain exchanges to be considered "like kind" and allowable. These include life insurance for life insurance, life insurance for non-qualified annuity, life insurance for endowment, endowment for non-qualified annuity, endowment for endowment, and non-qualified annuity for non-qualified annuity. They also will allow multiple numbers of existing contracts to be changed into a single newer contract. It does not work in reverse. A single existing contract can not be exchanged in for multiple newer contracts, per the IRS rules and regulations.

Annuity

An annuity is an investment contract that an insurance company sells to individuals. This agreement promises that it will make a regular series and dollar amount of payments to the buyer. This can be either for the rest of his or her life or for a set amount of time. The payments out are typically made after the individual retires.

Annuities have a long past that began in the Roman Empire. Roman citizens could purchase annual contracts from the Roman Emperor. The empire would then make annual payments to the citizens for the remainder of their lives. European governments revived the sale of annuities in the 1600s. They sold lump sum contracts to investors to help pay for expensive wars.

These investors also received a number of prearranged payments back from the governments that sold them. Annuities in America started as a way to support church ministries. 1912 saw the first annuity contract that was offered to the general American public by a Pennsylvania life insurance firm. These contracts continued to evolve and grow throughout the 1950s until they became commonplace in the 1980s.

Annuities offer certain tax advantages to their owners. Annuity holders only pay taxes on their contributions when they begin to take withdrawals or distributions from the funds. Every annuity contract is tax deferred. This signifies that investment earnings in such annuity accounts continue to grow tax deferred until the owners withdraw them. This also means that annuity earnings may not be taken out without paying a penalty until the owner reaches the set age of 59 1/2.

There are two general types of annuities contracts. Fixed annuities pledge to provide a guaranteed payment amount. Variable annuities do not make this guarantee. They do offer the possibility of earning higher returns in the variable annuity. Experts consider either type of annuity to be a safe but low yielding investment vehicle.

Annuities have a specific purpose. Companies developed them in order to insure the owner against the possibility of living longer than his or her retirement income. This is known as superannuation. The idea behind annuities is to help offset this risk of outliving retirement funds.

Annuities are popular with conservative investors because they continue to make payments until the holder dies. Even when the payments surpass the amount that remains in the annuity, the payments continue to be made. They are always counted as retirement savings vehicles.

The two phases of annuities are the accumulation and the distribution periods. During the accumulation phase, owners do one of two things. They can make a large lump sum payment into the annuity. They may also make regular payments into the contract. If the owner dies in this accumulation period, the heirs are given the amount of money that the owner paid into the annuity contract. Taxes owed would include estate taxes and regular income taxes.

When the owner reaches the retirement age, annuitization happens and distribution begins. At this point, the accumulated amounts convert into annuity units. The owner is changing the lump sum amount in the contract for the guaranteed series of payments. At this point he or she no longer has access to the large single amount in the account. The guaranteed income for life begins in this distribution phase.

Owners can receive their benefits as one of several options. Straight Life contracts pay calculated sums that are only based on the owner's life expectancy. These payments stop when the owner dies even if a lesser amount than the contract value is distributed. Life with Period Certain option makes payments for a minimum amount of time up to the death of the owner. Joint Life option pays benefits until both owners have died. Joint Life with Period Certain option gives payments for a guaranteed minimum amount of time until both owners have died.

Bear Market

Bear markets are periods in which stock markets drop for an extended amount of time. These pullbacks typically run to twenty percent or even greater amounts of the underlying stock values. Bear markets are the direct opposites of bull markets, when prices rise for extended amounts of time.

Bear markets and their accompanying drastic drops in stock share prices are commonly caused by declining corporate profits. They can also result from the correction of a too highly valued stock market, where stock prices prove to be overextended and decline to more historically fair values. Bear markets commonly begin when investors become frightened by lower earnings or too high values for their stocks and begin selling them. When many investors sell their holdings at a single time, the prices drop, sometimes substantially. Declining prices lead still other investors to fear that their money that they have invested in the stock market will be lost too. This motivates them to sell out through fear. In this way, the vicious cycle down progresses.

There have been many instances of bear markets in the United States since the country began over two hundred years ago. Perhaps the greatest example of an extended bear market is that found in the 1970's. During these years, stocks traded down and then sideways for more than a full decade. These kinds of encounters keep potential buyers out of the markets. This only fuels the fire of the bear market and keeps it going, since only a few buyers are purchasing stocks. In this way, the selling continues, as sellers consistently outnumber buyers in the stock exchanges.

For long term investors, bear markets present terrific opportunities. A person who is buying stocks with the plan to keep them for tens of years will find in a bear market the optimal sale price point and time to purchase stocks. Though many individual investors become frenzied and sell their stocks continuously during a bear market, this is exactly the wrong time to sell them.

Bear markets provide savvy investors with the chance to seek out solid companies and fundamentals that should still be strong ten to twenty years in the future. Good companies will still do well in the coming years, even if their share prices fall twenty or forty percent with the overall market. A company like Gillette that makes razors will still have a viable and dependable market going years down the road, even if the stock is unfairly punished by a bear market. Making money in a bear market requires investors to understand that a company's underlying core business has to be distinguished from its short term share price. In the near term, a company's fundamentals and stock prices do not always have much in common.

This means that a discounted price on a good company in a bear market is much like a periodic clearance sale at a person's favorite store. The time to buy the products heavily is while they are greatly discounted. The stock market is much the same. History has demonstrated on a number of different occasions that the stock prices of good companies will rebound to more realistic and fair valuations given some time.

Bond Market

A bond market is a financial market where investors buy and sell bonds. In practice this is mostly handled electronically over computers nowadays. There are two principal types of bond markets. These are primary markets where companies are able to sell new debt and secondary markets where investors are able to purchase and resell these debt securities. Companies generally issues such debt as bonds. These markets also trade bills, notes, and commercial paper.

The goal of the bond markets is to help private companies and public entities obtain funding of a long term nature. This market has generally been the domain of the United States that dominates it. The U.S. comprises as much as 44% of this bond market on a global basis.

There are five primary bond markets according to SIFMA the Securities Industry and Financial Markets Association. These include the municipal, corporate, mortgage or asset backed, funding, and government or agency markets. The government bond market comprises a significant component of this market thanks to its massive liquidity and enormous size. Because of the stability of U.S. and some international government bonds, other bonds are often contrasted with them to help determine the amount of credit risk.

This is because government bond yields from countries with little risk like the U.S., Britain, or Germany are traditionally considered to be free of default risk. Other bonds denominated in these various currencies provide greater yields as the borrowers are more likely to default than these central governments.

Bond markets often serve a useful secondary function to reveal interest rate changes. This is because the values of bonds are inversely related to the interest rates which they pay. This helps investors to measure what the true cost of obtaining funding really is. Companies which are perceived to be riskier will have to pay higher interest rates on their bonds than companies believed to have strong and stable credit and repayment abilities. When companies or government entities are unable to make a partial or full payment on their bonds, this becomes a default.

When a company or a government needs to raise money and does not want to issue stock, it can sell bonds. These are contracts the issuers who are the borrowers make with investors who function as lenders. When investors purchase such instruments, they lend money to the issuing organization (company or government). The issuer of the bond promises to repay the original investment back along with interest in the future.

Bonds traded on these markets have many elements in common, whichever type of market they represent. All bonds have a face value. This is the amount of money which a bond would be valued at when it matures and the amount on which interest payments are based. They also have coupon rates that represent the interest rate which the issuer of the bond pays in its interest payments.

The coupon dates turn out to be the times when the issuer will pay its interest payments. Issue prices are the amounts for which the issuer sells the bond in the first place. The maturity date proves to be the exact date when the bond would be repaid. At this time, the issuer of the bond would pay the bond's face value to the bond holder.

Though a holder of a bond might keep it until maturity, this is often not the case. Many investors buy and sell them on the bond markets as their needs dictate. It is possible to sell a bond at a premium when the market value becomes greater than the original face value. Investors could also sell them at a discount to their original face value as the market price declines.

Bonds

Bonds are also known as debt instruments, fixed income securities, and credit securities. A bond is actually an IOU contract where the terms of the bond, interest rate, and date of repayment are all particularly defined in a legal document. If you buy a bond at original issue, then you are literally loaning the issuer money that will be repaid to you at a certain time, along with periodic interest payments.

Bonds are all classified under one of three categories in the United States. The first of these are the highest rated, safest category of Federal Government debt and its associated agencies. Treasury bills and treasury bonds fall under this first category. The second types of bonds are bonds deemed to be safe that are issued by companies, states, and cities. These first two categories of bonds are referred to as investment grade. The third category of bonds involves riskier types of bonds that are offered by companies, states, and cities. Such below investment grade bonds are commonly referred to as simply junk bonds.

Bonds' values rise and fall in directly opposite correlation to the movement of interest rates. As interest rates fall, bonds rise. When interest rates are rising, bonds prices fall. These swings up and down in interest rates and bond prices are not important to you if you buy a bond and hold it until the pay back, or maturity, date. If you choose to sell a bond before maturity, the price that it realizes will be mostly dependent on what the interest rates prove to be like at the time.

Bonds' investment statuses are rated by the credit rating agencies. These are Standard & Poor's, Moody's, and Fitch Ratings. All bond debt issues are awarded easy to understand grades, such as A+ or B. In the last few years of the financial crisis, these credit rating agencies were reprimanded for having awarded some companies bonds' too high grades considering the risks that the companies undertook. This was especially the case with the bonds of banks, investment companies, and some insurance outfits.

Understanding the bond markets is a function of comprehending the yield curves. Yield curves turn out to be pictorial representations of a bond's interest rate and the date that it reaches maturity, rendered on a graph. Learning to understand and read these curves, and to figure out the spread between such curves, will allow you to make educated comparisons between various issues of bonds.

Some bonds are tax free. These are those bonds that are offered by states and cities. Such municipal bonds, also known as munis, help to raise funds that are utilized to pay for roads, schools, dams, and various other projects. Interest payments made on these municipal bonds are not subject to Federal taxes. This makes them attractive to some investors.

Cap Rate

Cap rate refers to the real estate property and its rate of return. Investors figure this out by utilizing the income which they anticipate the property will generate. The cap rate is also referred to as the capitalization rate. Realtors utilize it to gauge how much return investors will realize on their investments.

The way people determine this cap rate is by using an easy to understand formula. Investors take the property's NOI net operating income and divide it by the current fair market value of the property. This NOI turns out to be the annual return less all operating costs. The capitalization rate formula can be written as Capitalization Rate = Net Operating Income / Current Market Value. Investors and realtors express it as a percentage.

Investors consider the cap rate to be very helpful because it summarizes information regarding real estate investments. It is also simple to understand. This important rate discerns the profitability of a given piece of property. In order for it to remain consistent, the net operating income and current market value have to be constant compared to each other. If the NOI goes up when market value remains constant, the capitalization rate rises. If instead market value increases while NOI remains the same, then this rate will go down.

Real estate investments only stay profitable if the NOI goes up at the same rate as or a greater rate than the increase in the value of the property. This is another way that the capitalization rate is helpful. It can be employed to track the performance of real estate investments through time to learn if their performance is increasing. When the rate declines instead, investors may decide to sell the property so that they can reinvest the capital in some other place.

The cap rate is especially practical because it allows individuals to measure different investments in property. It permits them to compare and contrast a number of different investment possibilities against each other. Sometimes it is not easy to compare operating income or market values of radically different properties. Comparing percentages to one another is simple and intuitive. The rate is at its most useful when either the current market value or NOI are similar. This is because investments where the cost is vastly different can create a variety of other considerations that interfere with effective comparison.

Many times investors will come up with a minimum capitalization rate which they are willing to take so that the investment is practical. They might set 12% as their minimum rate. This helps them to sift through the various possibilities to rule out the ones that do not measure up to their desired minimum.

Investors may also employ the capitalization rate to figure out the amount of time it will take for the investment to reach its payback point. They can find the payback period by taking 100 and dividing it by the capitalization rate. This will provide an estimate of the payback period and not a fixed number. Most investments will see their capitalization rate change during significant amounts of time.

Another useful way of determining the value for a real estate investment is to utilize direct capitalization. To find this number, investors simply divide their NOI by the cap rate. This provides them with the capital cost of the real estate investment in question.

Investors should realize that the capitalization rate is not so helpful for shorter time frame investments as it is for longer ones. Figuring up NOI requires some time to determine a cash flow number that is reliable.

Capital Appreciation

Capital appreciation refers to the increase in an asset's value. This gain is based on the increase in the market price of the asset. It primarily happens as the asset which an investor backed goes for a greater market price than the investor first paid for the asset in question. The part of the asset which is considered to be capital appreciating covers the entire market value which exceeds the cost basis, or original amount invested.

There are two principle sources of returns on investment. The largest of these is typically the capital appreciating component of the return. The other return source is from dividends or interest income. The total return of an investment results from the inclusion of both the appreciation of capital and the dividend return or interest income.

There are a wide variety of reasons why capital appreciation can occur in the first place. These differ from one asset class or market to the next, but the idea is the same. With financial assets like stocks or hard assets such as real estate, this can occur similarly.

Examples of this appreciation of capital abound. If a stock investor buys shares for $20 a piece while the stock provides a yearly dividend of $2, then the dividend yield is ten percent. A year after this, if the stock is trading at $30 and the investor obtained the $2 dividend, then the investor has enjoyed a return of $10 in capital appreciating since the stock increased from $20 to $30. The percent return of the stock price increase amounts to a capital appreciating level of 50 percent. With the $2 dividend return, the dividend yield is another ten percent. That makes the combined capital appreciation between the stock price increase and the dividend payout $12, or 60 percent. This stunning total return would please most any investor in the world.

A variety of different causes can lead to this appreciation of capital for a given asset. A generally rising trend can support the prices of the investment. These can come from such macroeconomic factors as impressive GDP growth or accommodative policies of the Federal Reserve in lowering their benchmark interest rates. It might also be something more basic having to do with the company that issued the stock itself. Stock prices could rise when the firm is outperforming the prior expectations of analysts. The real estate value of a house or other property could increase because it has good proximity to upcoming new developments like major roads, shopping centers, or good schools.

Mutual funds are another investment example which seeks out capital appreciation. The funds hunt for investments which will likely increase in value because of their undervalued but solid fundamentals or because they have earnings which outperform analysts' expectations. It is true that such investments often entail larger risks than those alternatives picked for income generation or preservation of capital, as with municipal bonds, government bonds, or high dividend paying stocks.

This is why those funds which focus on capital appreciation are deemed to be more appropriate for those investors who have a higher tolerance for risk. Growth funds are usually called capital appreciation investments since they pour their funds into company stocks which are rapidly expanding and boosting their shareholder values at the same time. They do employ capital appreciation as their primary investment strategy to meet the expectations of lifestyle and retirement investors.

Capital Gains

Capital gains refer to profits that arise when you sell a capital asset like real estate, stocks, and bonds. These proceeds must be above the purchase price to qualify as capital gains. A capital gain is also the resulting difference between a low buying price and a high selling price that leads to a financial gain for investors. The opposite of capital gains are capital losses, which result from selling such a capital asset at a price lower than for what you purchased it. Capital gains can pertain to investment income that is associated with tangible assets like financial investments of bonds and stocks and real estate. They may also result from the sale of intangible assets that include goodwill.

Capital gains are also one of the two principal types of investor income. The other is passive income. With capital gains' forms of income, large, one time amounts are realized on an asset or investment. There is no chance for the income to be continuous or periodic, as with passive income. In order to realize another capital gain, another asset must be purchased and acquired. As its value rises, it can also be sold to lock in another capital gain. Capital gain investments are generally larger amounts, though they only pay one time.

Capital gains have to be reported to the Internal Revenue Service, whether they belong to a business or an individual. These capital gains have to be designated as either short term gains or long term gains. This is decided by how long you hold the asset before choosing to sell it. When an asset with a gain is held longer than a year, the capital gain is long term. If it is held for a year or less time frame, such a capital gain proves to be short term.

When an individual or business' long term capital gains are greater than long term capital losses, net capital gains exist. This is true to the point that these gains are greater than net short term capital losses. Tax rates on these capital gains are lower than on other forms of income. Up to 2010's conclusion, the highest capital gains tax rates for the majority of investors proves to be fifteen percent. Those whose incomes are lower are taxed at a zero percent rate on their net capital gains.

When capital gains are negative, or are actually capital losses, the losses may be deducted form your tax return. This reduces other forms of income by as much as the yearly limit of $3,000. Additional capital losses can be carried over to future years when they exceed $3,000 in any given year, reducing income for tax purposes in the future. These capital gains and losses should be reported on the IRS' Schedule D for capital gains and losses.

Capital Loss

Capital Loss refers to a type of loss that companies or individuals experience as one of their capital assets decreases by value. This includes a real estate or investment asset. The loss only becomes realized when the asset itself sells for less than the price for which it was originally purchased. Another way of looking at these capital losses is that they represent the difference from the asset's purchase price and the asset's selling price. In other words, for it to be a loss the selling price must be less than the original price. As an example, when investors purchase a home for $300,000 and then sell the same home six years later for only $260,000, they have taken a capital loss amounting to $40,000.

Where income taxes are concerned, capital losses often offset capital gains. Capital losses in fact reduce the personal or business income in a like dollar for dollar amount. When net losses are higher than $3,000, then the overage amount can not be applied. Instead, this amount higher than net $3,000 simply carries over against any other gains or taxable income to the following year when they will similarly offset capital gains and income. When losses are multiple thousands, they continue to carry forward as many years as it takes for them to be fully exhausted.

Both capital losses and capital gains will be reported using a Form 8949. This form helps taxpayers to determine if the sale dates allow for the transactions to be counted as long term or short term losses or gains. When such transactions are deemed to be short term gains, they become taxable by the individual's ordinary income tax rates. These ranged from only 10 percent to 39.6 percent as of 2015. This is why the shorter term losses when paired off against shorter term gains give significant tax advantages to higher income earning individuals. It benefits them when they have earned profits by selling off any asset or assets in under a year from original purchase point.

With longer term capital gains, investors become taxed by rates of zero percent, 15 percent, or 20 percent. This occurs when they take a gain which results from a position they possessed for over a year. Such capital gains also can only be offset by capital losses which they realize after holding the investments for over a year. It is also on form 8949 that these assets become reportable. Here investors list out both the gross proceeds from the sales and assets' cost basis. The two figures are compared to determine if the total sales equate to a loss, gain, or wash. Such losses become reported on Schedule D. Here the taxpayer is able to ascertain the amount that may be utilized to lower overall taxable income.

These wash sale rules can be confusing to individuals without an example. Consider an investor who dumps his IBM stock on the last day of November in order to realize a loss. The taxing authority of the Internal Revenue Service will disallow such a capital loss if the exact stock was bought again on the day of December 30th or before this. This is because investors have to wait at least 31 days before such a security can be repurchased then sold off once more in order to realize another loss.

Yet the regulation does not affect sales and re-buys of different mutual funds that possess similar positions and holdings. As an example, $10,000 worth of Vanguard Energy Fund shares may be entirely reinvested in the Fidelity Select Energy Portfolio at any point. This would not forfeit the investors' ability to recognize another loss even as they continue to own an equity portfolio (through the mutual fund) that is similar to their earlier mutual fund holdings.

Capital Stock

A business' capital stock is the up front capital that the founders of the firm invest in or put into the company. This capital stock also proves useful as security for a business' creditors. This is because capital stock may not be taken out of the business to disadvantage the creditors in question. Such stock is separate from a business' assets or property that can rise and fall in value and amount.

A company's capital stock is segregated into shares. The complete number of such shares have to be detailed when the business is founded. Based on the entire sum of money that is put into the company when it is started up, each share will possess a particular face value that must be declared.

This value is referred to as par value of the individual shares. These par values are the minimum sums of money that may be issued and sold in stock shares by the business. It is similarly the capital value representation in the business' own accounting. In some countries, these shares do not contain any par value period. In this case, the capital stock shares would be termed non par value stock. Such shares literally represent a portion of an ownership in the business in question. These businesses may then declare various classes of shares. All of these could have their own privileges, rules, and share values.

The owning of such capital stock shares is proven by the possession of a certificate of stock. These stock certificates prove to be legal documents that detail the numbers of shares each shareholder owns. Other particular data of the capital stock shares, including class of shares and par value, is similarly detailed on these certificates.

These owners of the firm in question may decide that they need more capital in order to invest in additional projects that the company has in mind. Besides this, they might decide that they want to cash out some of their own holdings in order to release a portion of capital for their own private needs. They can do this by selling all or some of their capital stock to many partial owners. The ownership of one such share gives the share owner an ownership stake in the company. This includes such privileges as a tiny portion of any profits that may be paid out as dividends, as well as a small part of any decision making powers.

These shares sold from the capital stock each represent a single vote. The owners could decide to offer various classes of shares that could then have differing rights of voting. By owning a majority of the shares, the owners can out vote all of the little shareholders combined. This permits the original owners to maintain effective control of their company even after issuing shares of their capital stock to investors.

Cash Flow

Cash Flow is either an incoming revenue or outgoing expense stream that affects the value of any cash account over time. Inflows of cash, or positive cash flows, typically result from one of three possible activities, including operations, investing, or financing for businesses or individuals. Individuals are also able to realize positive cash flows from gifts or donations.

Negative cash flow is also called cash outflows. Outflows of cash happen because of either expenses or investments made. This is the case for both individuals' finances, as well as for those of businesses.

Where both individual finances and business corporate finances are concerned, positive cash flows are required to maintain solvency. Cash flows could be demonstrated because of a past transaction like selling a business product or a personal item or investment. They might also be projected into a future time for some consideration that a company or individual anticipates receiving and then possibly spending. No person or corporation can survive for long without cash flow.

Positive cash flow is essential for a variety of needs. Sufficient cash flow allows for money for you to pay your personal bills and creditors. It also allows a business to cover the costs of employee payroll, suppliers' bills, and creditors' payments in a timely fashion. When individuals and businesses lack sufficient cash on hand to maintain their budget or operations, then they are named insolvent. Lasting insolvency generally leads to personal or corporate bankruptcy.

For businesses, statements of cash flows are created by accountants. These demonstrate the quantity of cash that is created and utilized by a corporation in a certain time frame. Cash flows in this definition are calculated by totaling net income following taxes with non cash charges like depreciation. Cash flow is able to be assigned to either a business' entire operations or to one particular segment or project of the company. Cash flow is often considered to be an effective measurement of a business' ongoing financial strength.

Cash flows are also used by business and individuals to ascertain the value or return of a project or investment. The numbers of cash flows in to and out of such projects and investments are often utilized as inputs for indicators of performance like net present value and internal rate of return. A problem with a business' liquidity can also be determined by measuring the entire entity's cash flow.

Many individuals prefer investments that yield periodic positive cash flow over ones that pay only one time capital gains. High yielding dividend stocks, energy trusts, and real estate investment trusts are all examples of positive cash flow investments. Real estate properties can also be positive cash flow yielding investments when they provide greater amounts of rental income than their combined monthly mortgage payments, maintenance expenses, and property management upkeep costs and outflows total.

Closed End Funds

Closed end funds refer to those investment companies which are publicly traded and regulated by the SEC Securities and Exchange Commission. They are similar to mutual funds in some ways. Both represent investment funds which are pooled and overseen by a portfolio manager. The closed end varieties raise fixed amounts of capital. They do this in IPO initial public offerings. Such funds will then be established and structured, listed on a stock exchange, and finally then traded, bought, and sold as a stock is on one of the exchanges.

Other names for these closed end funds are closed end mutual funds or closed end investments. These funds have things in common with the open end funds as well as characteristics which are unique to them and which set them apart from such ETF exchange traded funds and mutual funds.

Closed end funds are only able to raise their capital in a single instance by utilizing an IPO and issuing a set quantity of shares. Investors in this closed end operation will then buy the shares like stock. They do have an important difference from typical stocks. Their shares are actually a certain interest within a given portfolio of securities that an investment advisor will actively manage. Usually they focus on a chosen and particular sector, geographic area and market, or industry.

Stock prices of these closed end funds vary with the market supply and demand forces. They also fluctuate based on the changes in the values of the underlying assets or securities which the fund contains. While there are many of these particular closed end funds, among the biggest in the fund universe is the Eaton Vance Tax-Managed Global Diversified Equity Income Fund.

There are a number of important characteristics which the closed end and open end funds share in common. Management teams run their investment portfolios in the two cases. The two types similarly assess and collect their annual expense ratio. They also may both provide capital gains and income distributions to their stakeholders.

The differences between the two types of funds in this universe are important. While open ended funds have their own particulars of trading, the closed end funds will trade exactly like stocks on their respective exchanges. The open ended variants receive a value and pricing only one time per day at the end of trading. The closed end variety will be both priced and traded repeatedly all through the market trading days. The closed end funds need a broker service to sell or buy them. In marked contrast to this, investors in the open ended funds many times may buy and sell their relevant shares directly with the provider of the fund.

A closed end fund also has some unique characteristics in the ways that its shares become priced. There is a difference between the funds NAV net asset value and the trading price. The NAV will be figured up at regular intervals throughout the day by computers. The actual price for which they trade on exchanges becomes set only by demand and supply forces interacting on the exchange. The end-result of this unique set of features is that the closed end fund might actually trade at a discount or premium to the net asset value.

This might occur for several different reasons. Those funds which are closed ended might be concentrating on a sector in the markets which happens to be more popular, such as biotechnology or alternative energy sources and technology. This would allow sufficient interest from investors to bid up the price of the fund to a premium over its actual NAV. When such funds are run by a stock picker with a successful track record, they can trade for a premium. At the same time, when investor interest is insufficient or there is a negative profile of risk and return perceived on the fund, it will often trade for a discount to net asset value.

Collateralized Debt Obligations (CDO)

Collateralized Debt Obligations are one of the financial weapons of mass destruction that helped to derail the global financial system in the financial crisis of 2007-2010. They are literally securities that are supposed to be of investment grade. The backing of collateralized debt obligations proves to be pools of loans, bonds, and similar assets. These investments are rated by the main ratings agencies of Moody's, Standard and Poors, and Fitch rating companies.

The actual value of collateralized debt obligations comes from their asset backing. These asset backed securities' payments and values both derive from their portfolios of associated assets that are fixed income types of instruments. CDO's securities are divided into different classes of risk that are called tranches.

The senior most tranches are deemed to be the most secure forms of securities. Since principal and interest payments are given out according to the most senior securities first, the junior level tranches pay the higher coupon payments and interest rates to help reward investors who are willing to take on the greater levels of default risk that they assume.

The original CDO was only offered in 1987 by bankers for Imperial Savings Association that failed and became folded in to the Resolution Trust Corporation in 1990. This should have been a warning about collateralized debt obligations, but their popularity only grew apace during the following ten years. CDO's rapidly became the fastest expanding part of the synthetic asset backed securities market. There are several reasons for why this proved to be the case. The main one revolved around the returns of two to three percentage points greater than corporate bonds that possessed identical credit ratings.

CDO's also appealed to a larger number of investors and asset managers from investment trusts, unit trusts, and mutual funds, to insurance companies, investment banks, and private banks. Structured investment vehicles also made use of them to defray risk. CDO's popularity also had to do with the high profit margins that they made for their creators and sellers.

A number of different investors and economists have raised their voices against collateralized debt obligations, derivatives in general, and other asset backed securities. This includes both former IMF Head Economist Raghuram Rajan and legendary billionaire investor Warren Buffet. They have claimed that such instruments only increase and spread around the uncertainty and risk that surrounds these underlying assets' values to a larger and wider pool of owners instead of lessening the risk via diversification.

Though the majority of the investment world remained skeptical of their criticism, the credit crisis in 2007 and 2008 proved that these dissenters had merit to their views. It is now understood that the major credit rating agencies did not sufficiently take into account the massive risks that were associated with the CDO's and ABS's, such as a nationwide housing value collapse.

Because the value of collateralized debt obligations are forced to be valued according to mark to market accounting, where their values are immediately updated to the market value, they have declined dramatically in value on the banks' and others owners' balance sheets as their actual value on the market has plummeted.

Collateralized Mortgage Obligation (CMO)

Collateralized mortgage obligations are investments that contain home mortgages. These mortgages underlie the securities themselves. These CMO yields and results derive from the home mortgage loans' performance on which they are based. This is true with other mortgage backed securities as well.

Lenders sell these loans to an intermediary firm. Such an intermediary pools these loans together and issues certificates based on them. Investors are able to buy these certificates to earn the principal and interest payments from the mortgages. The payments these homeowners make go through the intermediary firm before finally reaching the investors who bought them.

The performance of collateralized mortgage obligations depends on the track record of the mortgage payers. What makes them different from other types of mortgage backed securities is that it is not only a single loan on which they are based. Rather they are categorized by groups of loans according to the payment period for the mortgages within the pool itself.

Issuers set up CMOs this way to try to reduce the effects of a mortgage being prepaid. This can often be a problem for investments based on only a single mortgage as owners refinance their loans and pay off the initial one on which the investment was based. With the CMOs, the risk of home owners defaulting is spread across a number of different mortgages and shared by many investors.

Tranches are the different categories within the mortgage pools on which the collateralized mortgage obligations are based. The tranches are often divided according to the mortgage repayment schedules of the loans. For each tranche, the issuer creates bonds with different interest rates and maturity dates. These CMO bonds can come with maturity dates of twenty, ten, five, and two years. The bondholders of each individual tranche receive the coupon or interest payments out of the mortgage pool. Principal payments accrue initially to those bonds in the first tranche which mature soonest.

The bonds on collateralized mortgage obligations turn out to be highly rated. This is especially the case when they are backed by GSE government mortgages and similar types of high grade loans. This means that the risk of default is low compared with other mortgage backed securities.

There are three types of groups who issue these CMOs. The FHLMC Federal Home Loan Mortgage Corporation issues many of them. Other GSE Government Sponsored Enterprises like Ginnie Mae provide them as well. There are also private companies which issue these CMOs. Many investors consider the ones issued by the government agencies to be less risky, but this is not necessarily the case. The government is not required to bail out the GSEs and their CMOs.

There are investors who choose to hold their CMO bonds until they mature. Others will re-sell or buy them using the secondary market. The prices for these investments on this market go up and down based on any changes in the interest rates.

The other most common type of mortgage backed securities besides these CMOs are pass through securities. Pass throughs are usually based on a single or few mortgages set up like a trust that collects and passes through the interest and principal repayments.

Commercial Paper

Commercial paper proves to be a corporation-issued short term form of debt instrument which is unsecured. This paper is generally used to finance such things as inventories, accounts receivable, and other short term liabilities. The maturity dates for commercial paper vary, but they do not typically run any more than 270 days. Such paper instruments are generally issued at discounts to their face value. These discounts take into account the market interest rates that are effective when the company issues its paper.

Because commercial paper does not come with any underlying collateral, it turns out to be unsecured corporate debt. This means that only those companies that boast debt ratings which are highest quality will be able to find takers easily. Other companies must float their paper debt issues at greater discounts. This makes the funds come at a higher cost. Large organizations issue these paper instruments in significant denominations of typically $100,000 or higher. The most usual buyers of these paper instruments are banks and financial institutions, other companies, money market funds, and wealthy investors.

Commercial paper offers significant advantages for the corporations who utilize it. One of the biggest is that they do not have to register these offerings with the SEC Securities and Exchange Commission if the paper reaches maturity within 270 days or before nine months pass. This makes it a cost effective and quick way to obtain finance. While companies do have up to 270 days before the SEC is involved, typical maturity time frames for this paper only average around 30 days.

There are some restrictions to the use of commercial paper. It's funds can only be utilized for current assets and inventories. They may not be employed to purchase fixed assets like new facilities or plants unless the SEC is involved.

The financial crisis that began to erupt in 2007 involved the commercial paper market in a significant way. When investors had fears that major companies like Lehman brothers had problems with their liquidity and financial condition, markets for commercial paper seized up. Companies lost their access to funding which was affordable and simple to obtain.

This market freezing also led to money market funds "breaking the buck." As major investors in these paper instruments, the funds suffered from the suspect health of firms whose issued paper caused their own fund values to drop below the standard $1. Up to this point, money market funds had been considered risk free for investors. Government backing and guarantees were required to restore order and functionality to these markets.

A company might need additional short time frame funds in order to pay for Christmas holiday season additional inventory. The company could issue paper for $20 million in needs at $20.2 million face value. This means investors will provide it with $20 million in funding and receive $200,000 as interest when the paper matures. It would amount to a 1% interest rate. If the paper is not redeemed at its initial maturity, the interest rate would adjust the amount of principal and interest the paper would return appropriately based on the number of days it remained outstanding.

Commodities

Commodities turn out to be items that are taken from the earth, such as orange juice, cattle, wheat, oil, and gold. Companies buy commodities to turn them into usable products like bread, gasoline, and jewelry to sell to other businesses and consumers. Individual investors purchase and sell them for the purposes of speculation, in an attempt to make a profit.

Commodities are traded through commodities brokers on one of several different commodities exchanges, such as COMEX, or the Commodities Mercantile Exchange, NYMEX, or the New York Mercantile Exchange, and NYBOT, or the New York Board of Trade, among others.

Commodities are traded with contracts using a great amount of leverage. This means that with a small amount of money, a great quantity of the commodity in question can be controlled and traded. For example, with only a few thousand dollars, you as an investor are able to control a contract of one thousand barrels of heating oil or one hundred ounces of gold.

As a result of this high leverage that you obtain, the amounts of money made or lost can be significant with only relatively small moves in the price of the underlying commodity. This leverage results from the fact that commodities are nearly always traded using margin accounts that lead to significant risks for the capital invested. For example, with gold contracts, each ten cent minimum price move represents a $10 per contract gain or loss.

Commodity trading strategies center around speculation on factors that will affect the production of a commodity. These could be related to weather, natural disasters, strikes, or other events. If you believed that severe hurricanes would damage a great portion of the Latin American coffee crop, then you would call your commodity broker and instruct them to buy as many coffee contracts as they had money in the account to cover.

If the hurricanes took place and coffee did see significant damage in the region, then the prices of coffee would rise dramatically as a result of the negative weather, causing the coffee harvest to be more valuable. Your coffee contracts would similarly rise in value, probably significantly.

A variety of commodities can be traded on the commodities exchanges. These include grains, metals, energy, livestock, and softs. Grains consistently prove to be among the most popular of commodities available to trade. Grain commodities are usually most active in the spring and summer. Grains include soybeans, corn, oats, wheat, and rough rice.

Metals commodities offer you the opportunity to take positions on precious metals such as gold and silver. Changes in the underlying prices of base metals may also be traded in this category. Metals include copper, silver, and gold.

Energy commodities that you can trade are those used for heating homes and fueling vehicles for the nation. With the energy complex you can trade on supply disruptions around the world or higher gas prices that you anticipate. Energy commodities available to you are crude oil, unleaded gas, heating oil, and natural gas.

Livestock includes animals that provide pork and beef. Because these are staple foods in most American diets, they provide among the more reliable pattern trends for trading. Pork bellies, lean hogs, and live cattle are all examples of tradable livestock commodities.

Softs are comprised of both food and fiber types of commodities. Many of these are deemed to be exotic since they are grown in other countries and parts of the earth. Among the soft markets that you can trade are sugar, coffee, cocoa, cotton, orange juice, and lumber.

Common Stock

Common stocks are shares in an underlying company that represent equity ownership in the corporation. They are also known as ordinary shares. These are securities in which individuals invest their capital. Common stock is the opposite of preferred stock.

While common stock and preferred stock both represent ownership in the company, there are many important differences between the two. Should a company go bankrupt, common stock holders are only given their money after preferred stock owners, bond owners, and creditors. Yet, common stock performs well, typically seeing greater levels of price appreciation than does preferred stock.

Common stock typically comes with voting rights, another feature that preferred stock does not have. These votes are used in electing the board of directors at the company's annual meeting, as well as in determining such things as company strategy, stock splits, policies, mergers and acquisitions, and the sale of the company. Preemptive rights in common stocks refer to owners with these rights being allowed to keep the same proportion of ownership in the company' stock, even if it issues additional stock.

Common stocks do not always pay dividends to share holders, as preferred stocks typically do. The dividends of common stocks are not pre-set or fixed. This means that the dividend returns are not completely predictable. Instead, they are based on a company's reinvestment policies, earnings results, and practices of the market in the valuing of the stock shares themselves.

Common shares have various other benefits. They are typically less expensive than are preferred stock shares. They are more heavily traded and readily available as well. The spreads between the buying and selling prices on them tend to be tighter as a result. Common stocks generally provide capital appreciation as the price of the shares rises over time, assuming that the company continues to do well and meet or exceed expectations. Dividends are often paid to common share holders when these things prove to be the case.

Common stocks can be purchased in any denominated amount. Round lots of common stocks are sold by even one hundred share amounts. This means that five hundred shares of common stock would be considered to be five lots of common stock.

Common stocks represent principally capital gains types of investments, as an investor is looking to buy them low and sell them at a higher price. This leads to a capital gain when the stock is sold at this greater level. The capital gain is the difference between the selling price and the purchasing price. Common stocks can also be cash flow types of investments when they pay a reliable stream of dividends every quarter. These income amounts are typically smaller than the one time amounts realized in capital gains, though they are obtained four times per year on a quarterly basis, or occasionally more often on a monthly basis.

Convertible Bond

A convertible bond is like a hybrid between a stock and a bond. Corporations issue these bonds which the bondholders may choose to convert into shares of the underlying company stock whenever they decide. Such a bond usually pays better yields than do shares of common stocks. Their yields are also typically less than regular corporate bonds pay.

Convertible bonds provide income to their investors just as traditional corporate bonds do. These convertibles also possess the unique ability to gain in price if the stock of the issuing company does well. The reasoning behind this is straightforward. Because the bond has the ability to be directly converted into stock shares, the security's value will only gain as the stock shares themselves actually rise on the market.

When the stock performs poorly, the investors do not have the ability to convert the convertible bond into shares. They only gain the yield as a return on the investment in this case. The advantage these bonds have over the company stock in these deteriorating conditions is significant.

The value of the convertible instrument will only drop to its par value as long as the company that issues it does not go bankrupt. This is because on the specified maturity date, investors will obtain back their original principal. It is quite correct to say that these types of bonds typically have far less downside potential than do shares of common stocks.

There are disadvantages as well as advantages to these convertible bonds. Should the issuer of the bond file for bankruptcy, investors in these kinds of bonds possess a lower priority claim on the assets of the corporation than do those who invested in debt which was not convertible. Should the issuer default or not make an interest or principal payment according to schedule, the convertibles will likely suffer more than a regular corporate bond would. This is the flip side to the higher potential to appreciate which convertibles famously possess. It is a good reason that individuals who choose to invest in single convertible securities should engage in significant and extended research on the issuer's credit.

It is also important to note that the majority of these convertible bonds can be called. This gives the issuer the right to call away the bonds at a set share price. It limits the maximum gain an investor can realize even if the stock significantly outperforms. This means that a convertible security will rarely offer the identical unlimited gain possibilities which common stocks can.

If investors are determined to do the necessary research on an individual company, they can purchase a convertible bond from a broker. For better convertible diversification, there are numerous mutual funds which invest in only convertible securities. These funds are provided by a variety of major mutual fund companies.

Some of the biggest are Franklin Convertible Securities, Vanguard Convertible Securities, Fidelity Convertible Securities, and Calamos Convertible A. Several ETF exchange traded funds provide a similar convertible diversification with lower service charges. Among these are the SPDR Barclays Capital Convertible Bond ETF and the PowerShares Convertible Securities Portfolio.

It is important to know that the bigger convertible securities portfolios such as the ETFs track have a tendency to match the performance of the stock market quite closely in time. This makes them similar to a high dividend equity fund. Such investments do offer possible upside and diversification when measured against typical holdings of bonds. They do not really offer much in the way of diversification for individuals who already keep most of their investment dollars in stocks.

Corporate Bonds

Corporate bonds are debt securities that a company issues and sells to investors. Such corporate bonds are generally backed by the company's ability to repay the loan. This money is anticipated to result from successful operations in the future time periods. With some corporate bonds, the physical assets of a company can be offered as bond collateral to ease investors' minds and any concerns about repayment.

Corporate bonds are also known as debt financing. These bonds provide a significant capital source for a great number of businesses. Other sources of capital for the companies include lines of credit, bank loans, and equity issues like stock shares. For a business to be capable of achieving coupon rates that are favorable to them by issuing their debt to members of the public, a corporation will have to provide a series of consistent earnings reports and to show considerable earnings potential. As a general rule, the better a corporation's quality of credit is believed to be, the simpler it is for them to offer debt at lower rates and float greater amounts of such debt.

Such corporate bonds are always issued in $1,000 face value blocks. Practically all of them come with a standardized structure for coupon payments. Some corporate bonds include what is known as a call provision. These provisions permit the corporation that issues them to recall the bonds early if interest rates change significantly. Every call provision will be specific to the given bond.

These types of corporate bonds are deemed to be of greater risk than are government issued bonds. Because of this perceived additional risk, the interest rates almost always turn out to be higher with corporate bonds. This is true for companies whose credit is rated as among the best.

Regarding tax issues of corporate bonds, these are pretty straight forward. The majority of corporate bonds prove to be taxable, assuming that their terms are for longer than a single year. To avoid taxes until the end, some bonds come with zero coupons and redemption values that are high, meaning that taxes are deferred as capital gains until the end of the bond term. Such corporate debts that come due in under a year are generally referred to as commercial paper.

Corporate bonds are commonly listed on the major exchanges and ECN's like MarketAxess and Bonds.com. Even though these bonds are carried on the major exchanges, their trading does not mostly take place on them. Instead, the overwhelming majority of such bonds trading occurs in over the counter and dealer based markets.

Among the various types of corporate bonds are secured debt, unsecured debt, senior debt, and subordinated debt. Secured debts have assets underlying them. Senior debts provide the strongest claims on the corporation's assets if the venture defaults on its debt obligations. The higher up an investor's bond is in the firm's capital structure, the greater their claim will ultimately be in such an unfortunate scenario as default or bankruptcy.

Credit Default Swaps

A credit default swap, or CDS, is a contract exchange that transfers between two parties the exposure of credit to fixed income products. Two parties are involved in this exchange. The purchaser of a credit default swap obtains protection for credit. The seller of this credit default swap actually guarantees the product's credit worthiness. In this process, the default risk moves from the owner of the fixed income security over to the party that sells the swap.

In these CDS transfers, the purchaser of the protection gives a series of fees or payments to the seller. This is also known as the spread of the Credit Default Swap. The party selling the protection gets paid off in exchange for this, assuming that a loan or bond type of credit instrument suffers from a negative credit event.

In the most basic forms, Credit Default Swaps prove to be two party contracts arranged between sellers and buyers of credit protection. These Credit Default Swaps will address a reference obligor or reference entity. These are typically governments or companies. The party being referenced is not involved in the contract as a party or even necessarily aware of its existence. The purchaser of such protection then pays pre defined quarterly premiums, or the spread, to the party who is selling the protection.

Should the entity that is referenced then default, the seller of the protection pays the face value of the instrument to the buyer of the protection against a physical transfer of the bond. Such settlements can also be accomplished by auction or in cash. Defaults in Credit Default Swaps are called credit events. These defaults might include a bankruptcy, restructuring of the referenced entity, or a failure to make payment.

Credit Default Swaps are much like insurance on credit. The difference between them and such insurance lies in the fact that a CDS is not regulated like life insurance or casualty insurance is. Besides this, investors are capable of purchasing or selling this type of protection without having any such debt of the entity that is referenced. Resulting naked credit default swaps permit investors to engage in speculation on issues of debt and credit worthiness of entities that are referenced. These naked Credit Default Swaps actually make up the majority of the CDS market.

The majority of Credit Default Swaps prove to be in the ten to twenty million dollar range. They typically have maturities ranging from one to ten years. The Credit Default Swap market is mostly unregulated and turns out to be the largest financial market on earth.

These CDS products were actually created in the early part of the 1990's. The market for them grew dramatically beginning in 2003. By the conclusion of 2007, the total amount of them in existence proved to be an astonishing $62.2 trillion dollars. This amount declined to $38.6 trillion in the wake of the financial crisis at the conclusion of 2008. Since then, it has been growing alarmingly again. Critics of Credit Default Swaps have consistently referred to them as financial weapons of mass destruction, capable of blowing up the financial system and world economies in the process.

Credit Derivatives

Credit derivatives refer to bilateral contracts which are privately held. These contracts permit the holders to manage their credit risk exposure. Such derivatives turn out to be financial assets. Examples of the better-known ones in the derivatives universe are swaps, forward contracts, and options. The price of these is necessarily based upon the credit risk of economic entities like governments, companies, or private investors. This means that banks which are worried about one of their customers not being capable of repaying their loan are able to purchase protection against such a potential loss in default. They do this by keeping the loan on their books at the same time as they transfer the credit risk off to a third party more commonly referred to as the "counter party."

Such credit derivatives are only one of numerous different kinds of financial instruments available to investors and financial institutions today. With these derivatives, they are merely instruments whose existence derives from underlying financial instruments. The value which underlies them comes from a stock or other asset.

Two different principal forms of derivatives exist. These are calls and puts. Calls provide the right but not obligation to purchase a stock for a pre-set price called the strike price. Puts deliver the right but not obligation to sell particular stocks for pre-arranged strike prices. With either calls or puts, investors are obtaining insurance in case a stock price rises or falls. This makes every form of derivative product an insurance vehicle and particularly these credit derivative examples.

Numerous credit derivatives exist on the markets today. Among these are CDO Collateralized Debt Obligations, CDS Credit Default Swamps, credit default swap options, total return swaps, and credit spread forwards. Banks are allowed to utilize these complicated instruments in order to completely take away their default risk from even an entire loan portfolio. The financial institutions or banks pay a premium, or upfront fee, for this accommodation.

Considering a concrete example helps to make the credit derivatives concept clearer. Plants R Us borrows $200,000 off of a bank with a ten year repayment term. Because Plants R Us shows a poor credit history, they are forced to buy the bank a credit derivative in order to be able to receive the loan. The bank accepts this product which will permit them to transfer all of the default risk to a third counter party. This means that the counter party would be forced to deliver all unpaid interest and principal on the loan in the event that Plants R Us defaults on the said loan. For this guarantee, Plants R Us pays an annual fee to the counter party for their assumed risk. Should the Plants R Us not default on the loan, then the counterparty firm keeps the entire fee. This makes it a win-win-win situation for all three parties. The bank is protected against a default by Plants R Us, which gets to have its loan. The counter party collects the yearly fee. All parties gain and benefit from the arrangement.

Credit derivatives' values vary widely depending on several factors. These include the borrower's credit quality as well as the counter party's credit quality. The biggest concern comes down to the credit quality of the third party - counter party. If the counter party defaults or is otherwise unable to honor their commitments specified in the derivatives contract, then the financial institution will not get its payment for the loan principal and interest. The counter party would naturally no longer receive its annual premium payments any longer either. This is why the quality of credit for the counter party is so much more critical than is the credit quality of the borrower (Plants R Us in the example).

Credit Ratings Agencies

Credit Ratings Agencies are those companies whose purpose is to consider and report on the financial strength which firms and government agencies demonstrate. They report on national as well as international corporations and agencies in this capacity. Their reports are most interested in the ability of the entities in question to fulfill their obligations for both principal and interest repayments of their bonds and other kinds of debts. Besides this, the various ratings agencies carefully examine and review the conditions and terms on every debt issue.

The end result of the agencies' work is to release a credit rating on both the debt issues in particular and the debt issuers more generally. When they agencies have high confidence that the issuer will be able to meet their debt servicing of principal and interest as promised, they will issue a high credit rating. When the opposite is true, the credit rating will be lower. It is entirely possible for a particular issue of debt to receive a differing credit rating from the issuer. This heavily depends on the particular terms of the issuer.

The impacts of these debt issue ratings are enormous in the industry and for the specific issuers in question. Those debt issues that obtain the best credit ratings will receive the most attractive interest rates from the credit markets. This is because the confidence of investors in an entity's capability of making their various payment obligations comes down to the credit ratings agencies review, analyses and especially ratings. Since the interest rates which investors demand for a specific debt issue will be inversely correlated to the borrower's particular creditworthiness, weaker borrowers will have to pay more while the stronger ones will enjoy paying less.

In this way, the credit ratings agencies act on behalf of businesses in much the same capacity as the consumer credit bureaus do for individual consumers. Such credit scores which the credit bureaus develop for individual people will greatly impact the interest rates at which individuals are able to borrow money.

The downside to these credit ratings agencies and their work is that they have been made the scapegoat for company and government defaults in recent years. Their research quality in particular has been the target of heavy criticism from observers and analysts who point out companies which they rated highly suddenly collapsed. Governments in Europe on which they provided high credit ratings defaulted or almost defaulted on their debts, as with Greece in particular.

This caused third party observers to argue that the various credit ratings agencies are actually poor at financial forecasting, at uncovering growing and negative trends for the debt issuers they follow, and also are overly late in revising down their ratings. Besides this, critics point to the many conflicts of interest of the ratings agencies. This is because the debt issuers are able to pick out and pay the ratings agencies for the reviews of their bonds. In a survey conducted in 2008, 11 percent of the various investment professionals surveyed by the CFA Institute responded that they had observed personally instances where the major ratings agencies had actually upgraded their given ratings on bonds when they were pressured by the debt issuers in question.

There are only three firms today which dominate the space, and this is part of the problem. The Wall Street Journal provided the ratings shares of the big 3 agencies in their 2011 report. Of the 2.8 million ratings they issue collectively (with the other seven minor agencies), S&P 500 controls the greatest market share with 42.2 percent. Moody's holds 36.9 percent of the market. Fitch rounds out the top three with 17.9 percent.

The article claimed that fully 95 percent of all revenues in this industry were earned by the big three. Only 2.9 percent of the ratings issued came from the other seven firms. The other seven credit ratings agencies were A.M. Best, DBRS, Japan Credit Rating Agency, Rating and Investment Info., Egan-Jones Ratings, Morningstar Credit Ratings, and Kroll Bond Rating Agency.

Between the top two issuers Moody's and Standard & Poor's, they provide ratings for roughly 80 percent of all municipal and corporate bond issues. They are typically regarded as a level higher than Fitch. One particular example speaks volumes. While Egan-Jones had downgraded the U.S. Federal government debt to the second highest rating years earlier, it was ignored largely by the markets and world. When Standard & Poor's took the same action by downgrading the Federal government of the United

States debt to AA+ on August 5th of 2011, this shook the world bond, currency, and stock markets. It demonstrates the clout S&P and Moody's especially enjoy over all of their various credit ratings agencies rivals.

Deferred Annuity

A Deferred Annuity refers to a specific kind of annuity contract. These types of annuities delay income payments (in the form of either a lump sum or installments) to the point where the investor chooses to obtain them. There are two principal stages in these kinds of annuities. These are the savings phase and the income phase. In the savings phase, individuals put money into the contract. The income phase is the one after the annuity becomes converted so that the payments are distributed as arranged. With deferred annuities there are several sub-types. These include fixed, variable, equity-indexed, and longevity.

A Fixed Deferred Annuity operates similarly to a CD Certificate of Deposit. The main difference lies in how the interest income must be claimed. With these annuities, it becomes long-term deferred until the owners take disbursements from the contract. These fixed contracts come with a guaranteed rate of interest that all funds earn. The insurance company stands behind the guarantee. These are attractive choices for those investors who are averse to risk and who do not require any interest income until after they turn 59 and ½ or older.

A variable Deferred Annuity is something like an assortment of mutual funds. With annuities, they refer to these as sub-accounts. Each owner has personal control over the investment risk he or she engages in through selecting particular sub-accounts which may cover both stocks and bonds. The returns on these investments will influence how well the annuity performs. For most investors, it benefits them more to purchase shares in several index mutual funds. This is because deferring taxes to retirement could mean that the owners will possibly pay higher taxes when they are retired than when they are working. The fees can also be as high as greater than three percent each year with many variable annuities.

Equity indexed annuities work much like the fixed annuities but also have variable annuity-like features. They possess two features. The first proves to be a guaranteed minimum return. The second is the ability to obtain a higher return than this by gaining from a formula which is based on one of the popular indices of the stock market like the S&P 500 or the Dow Jones Industrial Average. The downside to this type is that it typically comes with expensive surrender charges that can last over a ten to fifteen consecutive year long period.

Buying one of these last categories, the longevity annuity, is akin to obtaining insurance for a long life expectancy. It is helpful to consider a real life example to better understand how this works out in practice. An investor who is 60 might decide to pay in $150,000 to one of these longevity annuities. In exchange for this consideration, the insurance company which backs it will promise to pay out a set dollar amount of income for the rest of the holder's life beginning 25 years later at age 85. The advantage to this type of arrangement is that the retirees can then spend their other retirement assets because they feel comfortable that there will be a steady income stream that will support them guaranteed the rest of their lives. All income and taxes would be deferred to the distribution age when the money begins being disbursed.

It is important to realize with these annuities that any early withdrawals realized before the owners reach their legal retirement age will come with a full 10 percent penalty tax on top of the regular income taxes which the IRS will assess. The income tax rate would be based on the tax bracket of the individual when they receive the distribution.
These deferred annuities have many interesting (but often expensive) options and features which the buyers can obtain. Some of these include future income guarantees and death benefits.

Dividend Stocks

Dividend Stocks refer to stocks that pay especially generous and predictable shares of the corporate earnings out to their share holders. They are especially important for those investors who require dependable continuous streams of income off of their investment portfolios, such as retirees. This is why the optimal stock portfolio for those who are officially retired includes a strong and diverse mixture of industry-leading corporations which provide consistent, generous dividend yields.

These Dividend Stocks are famous for paying out significant stock dividends as a distribution on their earnings. They may pay this in the form of additional shares or as cash, depending on the wishes of the share holder in question. Sometimes the company will declare a stock dividend instead of a cash dividend, removing the ability of the shareholder to choose the form in which the dividend actually pays. When dividends become payable strictly as more stock, they are also known as stock splits.

For the companies that declare regular cash dividends of these Dividend Stocks, with each share stake holders have, they receive a set portion of the earnings from the corporation. This is literally being paid for simply owning the stock shares.

Consider a real world example to better understand how these Dividend Stocks work out in practice. Gillette, the world famous market leader in the shaving razors industry, may pay a dividend of $4 on an annual basis. Typically these dividends will be paid practically on a quarterly basis. This means four times each year Gillette would provide a $1 payout for each share of stock which the stake holders possess. If an investor owned 100 shares, he or she would receive four checks per year of $100 each check at approximately the conclusion of each quarter.

Most dividends from these Dividend Stocks come out in cash. Investors have the option to have them reinvested into additional company stock shares. Sometimes the corporation will provide a more advantageous reinvestment price than the current market prices to encourage such reinvesting of dividends in the company stock. These plans are called DRIPS (Dividend Re Investment Plans).

There are also occasional special dividends offered on an only one-time basis. They could be provided if the company wins a large and lucrative lawsuit, liquidates its share of an investment and receives a windfall payout, or sells part of the business to another firm for cash. These dividends can be made in cash, property, or stock share dividends.

There are several important dates with which Dividend Stocks' investors need to be familiar. These are declaration date, date of record, ex-dividend date, and payment date. Declaration date is the calendar day when the company's Board of Directors announces a dividend payout. This is the point where the firm adds a liability for the dividend payout to its company books. This means that it owes money (or shares) to the stake holders. This date will be the one when they announce both the date of record as well as the dividend payment date.

The date of record is the one where the corporation will review the appropriate records to determine who is holding the shares and is thus eligible for the dividends. Only holders of record will receive the dividend payment. The ex-dividend date is the day after which any investors who wish to receive dividends must own the shares. Only stake holders who possess shares on the day before the ex-dividend date get paid. Finally dividends are literally doled out on the payment date.

While most stock companies will pay out dividends on either a quarterly or half yearly basis, real estate investment trusts are structured differently. They pay out their dividends on an every-month basis as they receive monthly income from their various commercial, industrial, and/or residential properties.

Earnings Per Share (EPS)

Earnings per share refer to the given total of earnings that a company has for every share of the firm's stock that is outstanding. There are several formulas for calculating earnings per share. These depend on which segment of earnings are being considered. The FASB, or Financial Accounting Standards Board, makes corporations report such earnings per share on their income statement for all of the major components of such statements including discontinued operations, continuing operations, extraordinary items, and net income.

To figure up the basic net earnings per share formula, you only have to divide the profit for the year by the average number of common shares of stock. With discontinued operations, it is only a matter of taking the discontinued operations income and dividing it by the average number of common stock shares outstanding. Continuing operations earnings per share equal the continuing operations income over the average number of common shares. Extraordinary items works with the income from extraordinary items and divides it by the weighted average number of common shares.

Besides the basic earnings per share numbers, there are three different types of earnings per share. Last year's earning per share are the Trailing EPS. These are the only completely known earnings for a company. The Current earnings per share are the ones for this year. These are partially projections in the end until the last quarterly numbers are released. Finally, Forward earnings per share are earnings numbers for the future. These are entirely based on predictions.

Earnings per share calculations do not take into account preferred dividends on categories besides net income and continued operations. Such continuing operations and even net income earnings per share calculations turn out to be more complex as preferred share dividends are taken off of the top of net income before the earnings per share is actually calculated. Since preferred stock shares have the right to income payments ahead of common stock payments, any money that is given out as preferred dividends is cash which can not be considered to be potentially available for giving out to every share of the commonly held stock.

Preferred dividends for the present year are generally the only ones that are taken off of such income. There is a prevalent exception to this. If preferred shares prove to be cumulative then this means that dividends for the entire year are taken off, regardless of if they have been declared yet or not. Dividends that the company is behind on paying are not contemplated when the earnings per share is calculated.

Earnings per share as a financial measuring stick for a company are extremely important. In theory, this forms the underlying basis for the value of the stock in question. Another critical measurement of stock price is price to earnings value, also known as the PE ratio. This PE ratio is determined by taking the earnings per share and dividing them into the price of the stock. Earnings per share are useful in measuring up one corporation against another one, if they are involved in the same business segment or industry. They do not tell you if the stock is a good buy or not. They also do not reveal what the overall market thinks about the company. This is where the PE ratio is more useful.

Employee Stock Option (ESO)

Employee stock options are call options that are awarded privately rather than publicly. They turn out to be the most common form of equity compensation provided to employees of a business. Companies give out these options to their employees to provide them with an incentive to build up the market value of the company. These options may not be sold on the open markets.

An ESO provides the receiving employees with the right but not obligation to buy a preset quantity of shares of the company. The contract specifies a time frame within which these must be acquired before they expire worthless. The price they employees can buy them at is the current price which becomes the strike price. These time limits for using them are generally ten years. Companies spell all of these terms out in the options agreement.

These options are only valuable to the employee if the price of the company stock increases during the exercise time-frame. This is because the employees then are able to purchase the discounted shares at the same time as they sell them for the greater price on the market. The difference between the two prices represents their profit.

If the share price of the company declines, they are unable to use them and will see them eventually expire worthless. This is why companies utilize employee stock options instead of large salaries to encourage their employees. This provides the companies with great incentive to build up the value of the company. Three principle types of ESO exist in the form of non statutory, incentive, and reload employee stock options.

Non statutory employee stock options are also called non-qualified. These prove to be the normal kinds of ESOs. In such a contract, employees are not permitted to use these options during the vesting period. This vesting timeframe ranges from one to three years. When they are sold, the employee makes the spread between current price and strike price times the number of shares he or she sells. These types of ESOs become taxable at the employee's regular income tax level.

Graduated vesting in these options allows the employees to sell a percentage of the options such as maybe 10% in the first year. Each year another 10% would become available until the full 100% level is achieved by year ten. Incentive stock options are set up to lower taxes as much as possible. Employees can not exercise the option to buy the stock until after a year. They can not actually sell the stock until another year after buying it.

This type of option creates a risk that the stock price may decline over the year long holding time frame. The advantage to the employee is that these ISOs receive far better tax treatment. The tax rate defaults to the long term capital gains rate instead of the traditional full income tax rate. Upper level management are usually the ones who receive such tax advantageous ISOs from their companies.

The third type of employee stock options are called Reload ESOs. These begin their contract lives as non-statutory ESOs. The employees engage in their first exercise of the contract where they make money on the transaction. At this point, the employees who exercise are given a special reload of the employee stock option. In this process the company issues new options to the employee. The present market price at time of issue becomes the new strike price for the reloaded options. This way the employee is constantly re-incentivized to perform for the company.

Employee Stock Ownership Plan (ESOP)

An Employee Stock Ownership Plan refers to a type of retirement plan. They are also called by their acronym ESOP. These plans permit employing companies to either provide cash or stock shares directly to the employee benefits plan. These plans hold one account for every employee who participates in them. The stock shares that the employers contribute become vested over a pre-determined period of years.

Once they are partially or fully vested, employees are able to access them. It is important to note that with these ESOPs, employees never actually hold or purchase the shares of the stock directly when they are employees of the firm. Once the employee becomes retired, fired, disabled, or deceased, the stock shares become distributed.

One should never confuse an Employee Ownership Stock Plan with an employee stock option plan. These stock option plans are not really retirement plans. Rather they only provide the right to purchase the company stock for a given, pre-determined price in a certain time period.

One benefit that makes these Employee Stock Ownership Plans popular with providers and participants alike is their tax advantaged status. The reason they are considered to be qualified is because the company participating, the shareholder who sells, and the participants are each able to enjoy varying tax benefits. This is why these ESOPs are typically utilized by companies as part of their corporate financial strategy at the same time they are employed to encourage the employees to be sympathetic to the company stakeholders and their interests.

Without a doubt, the Employee Stock Ownership Plan is part and parcel of the compensation that employees enjoy from their company. This is why they are utilized to keep the employees working for the overall good of the company as a whole. They have a stake in the stock share price rising over time since they are part owners in the company stock.

These benefits from the Employee Stock Ownership Plan accrue to the employees at no upfront cost. The shares are kept for the receiving employees in a trust to ensure they grow safely to the point where the employee resigns or retires (or is fired).

These companies are actually employee-owned to some degree. Employee-owned corporations are those that have a majority of their shares in the hands of the company employees. This makes them cooperatives but for the fact that the firm's capital is unevenly distributed. Much of the time, such employee-owned corporations do not provide voting rights to all of the shareholders. Besides this, the senior-most employees and management will always have the distinct advantage of receiving a greater number of shares than the newer employees.

There are several other competing forms of employee ownership benefits. Among these are stock options, direct purchase plans, phantom stock, restricted stock, and stock appreciation rights. Stock options give their employees the chance to purchase shares of company stock for a set price in a fixed amount of time. A direct purchase plan permits employees to buy their shares in the company using their own after tax dollars.

Phantom stock delivers special cash bonuses in reward for superior employee results. The bonus amounts equal to the sale price of a certain quantity of stock shares. Restricted stock provides employees the ability to obtain shares either in the form of gift or by buying them, once they have met certain minimum employment period benchmarks. Stock appreciation rights provide employees with the ability to increase the value of a pre-assigned quantity of shares. Such shares typically become actually payable in the form of cash.

Euro Stoxx 50 Index

The Euro Stoxx 50 Index proves to be the leading European Blue-chip like index that comprises securities of mega companies from the Euro Zone. This index offers investors and financial institutions a vehicle for following and investing in the Blue chip type of sector leaders for the zone. It includes 50 stocks (as the name implies) drawn from 11 different Euro Zone member nations. These are economically important zone nations Spain, Portugal, the Netherlands, Luxembourg, Italy, Ireland, Germany, France, Finland, Belgium, and Austria.

This Euro Stoxx 50 Index has been licensed out to a wide range of financial institutions to be the basis of a great variety of investment products like ETF Exchange Traded Funds, Options on futures, Futures contracts, and structured products around the globe. Besides this master index of the Euro Stoxx 50 Index, it is subdivided into other indices. These include the following: Euro Stoxx 50 Subindex France, Euro Stoxx 50 Subindex Italy, and Euro Stoxx 50 subindex Spain which covers the national big 50 companies by market capitalization in each off the economic powerhouse countries of France, Italy, and Spain, respectively.

The operator of this important pan-Euro Zone Euro Stoxx 50 Index and business is the company STOXX Limited on behalf of Deutsche Boerse Group. They also offer international tradable and creative index concepts on other indices to numerous countries throughout the world. As of the end of June 2016, STOXX 50 and DAX have worked with iShares to create and offer two new exchange traded funds traded in Hong Kong. iShares exchange traded funds family are both managed and marketed by the BlackRock investment firm. They started trading these two new Euro STOXX 50 Index ETFs on the Hong Kong Stock Exchange at the conclusion of June 2016.

The components in the Euro Stoxx 50 Index are updated several times a year as appropriate to changing market capitalizations. As of the end of December 2016, the components included French firms oil and gas producer Total, health care and pharmaceuticals maker Sanofi, European and Global banking giant BNP Paribas, international insurance titan AXA, luxury personal household goods maker LVMH Moet, cosmetics international leader L'Oreal, chemical maker Air Liquide, industrial goods and services maker Schneider Electric, banking giant GRP Societe Generale, food and largest yogurt maker Danone Group, aircraft maker Airbus, construction materials producer Vinci, telecommunications provider Orange, industrial goods and services producer Safran, health care company Essilor International, construction and materials producer Saint Gobain, Real Estate company Unibail-Rodamco, Utilties giant Engie, and international media conglomerate Vivendi.

German components of the index were electronics and industrial goods giant Siemens, chemicals and pharmaceutical titan Bayer, leading technology firm SAP, chemicals international leader BASF, re-insurance leader Allianz, luxury car maker Daimler, telecommunications leader Deutsche Telekom, industrial goods and services provider Deutsche Post, healthcare leader Fresenius, luxury car maker BMW, insurance firm Muenchener Rueck, internationally known shoe and clothing manufacturer Adidas, utilities giant E.On, world's largest auto maker Volkswagen, and largest German financial institution Deutsche Bank.

Spanish components in the index were international banking conglomerates BCO Santander and BCO Bilbao Vizcaya Argentaria, telecommunications international behemoth Telefonica, utilities leader Iberdrola, and retailer Industria de Diseno Textil SA.

Dutch companies in the index include electronics and industrial goods maker Philips, Anglo-Dutch consumer products giant UniLever, financial services investment leader ING, technology leader ASML Holdings, and retailer Ahold Delhaize.

Italian components of the index were oil and gas producer and distributor ENI, largest Italian bank Intesa SanPaolo, and national utility company ENEL. The Irish component is construction and materials maker CRH. The Belgian component is alcohol and food giant Anheuser-Busch InBev. The Finish component is technology and cell phone maker manufacturer Nokia.

Expense Ratio

Expense ratio relates to the costs that a mutual fund incurs as it trades and does normal business. Typical mutual fund expense ratios include a number of different costs. Among these are management fees, transaction costs, custody costs, marketing fees, legal expenses, and transfer agent fees.

Management fees comprise those charges that the fund pays to the company which handles the portfolio management. They invest the fund's money as per the direction of the mutual fund board of directors. Management costs are typically the largest single portion of the mutual fund's expenses.

These fees commonly range from as little as .5% to as much as 2%. Lower fees are usually more advantageous for investors. This is because every dollar that goes to the management of the fund is not increasing the share holders' wealth. Some mutual fund types charge a higher amount in fees. International or global mutual funds will usually cost more than simple domestic market mutual funds. They justify these greater charges by the difficulty of managing an international portfolio.

Transaction costs include the fees that the fund pays to stock brokers. These are negotiated to extremely low rates such as a penny per share or even lower thanks to the enormous volumes that mutual funds trade. Those funds that are constantly purchasing and selling investments create significantly greater transacting costs for themselves and their investors. Higher turnover rates like this also can lead to larger capital gains taxes and other costs.

The investment holdings of a mutual fund must be kept by a custodian bank. This creates custody costs where these banks register the bonds, stocks, and other investments for the fund. Some of the banks do this electronically and others keep actual stock certificates in their vault storage.

Custodian banks also collect interest and dividend payments, maintain accounting for the various positions so gain/loss info is readily available to management, and handle stock splits and other transaction issues. These custodian costs prove to be a less significant percentage of expense ratios for the mutual funds.

Marketing fees for mutual funds come out of the money that the investors pool. This money is utilized to advertise the fund so they can raise additional investment dollars. More money in the fund means more management fees for the portfolio managers. These 12b-1 marketing fees are money that does not benefit an investor after the fund exceeds $100 million in net assets. A very small number of brokers actually refund such fees to their investors.

There are some legal expenses that mutual funds must incur in the course of normal operating business. These include for paperwork they are required by law to file for regulators like the SEC, specific licenses, incorporation, and other legal procedures. The majority of funds count such costs as a small amount of their overall expense ratio.

Transfer agent costs cover the expenses that arise when a shareholder cashes out or buys into the fund. Transfer agents must handle various account statements, paperwork, and money in the process. These agents take care of all the mundane daily paperwork for purchases, redemptions, and processing which keep the fund and other capital markets working.

There are various other costs that are not included in the mutual fund expense ratio but many experts feel should be. These include mutual fund sales loads. These fees are simply commissions that go into the pocket of the institution, company, or stockbroker that persuaded you to buy the mutual fund in the first place. Because of these and other high costs of many mutual fund expense ratios, some people prefer low cost index funds that involve very low management costs.

Financial Times Stock Exchange (FTSE)

The Financial Times Stock Exchange represents an enormous group of indices owned by the London Stock Exchange. The acronym originated in the days when it was half owned by the Financial Times newspaper and the LSE. Now this group is an entirely owned subsidiary of only the London Stock Exchange.

When individuals use the word FTSE, they are most commonly referring to the most important benchmark index of the group the FTSE 100. These 100 companies are the hundred largest British companies which the London Stock Exchange lists. As such the Blue Chip companies of the British economy represent the biggest companies by market capitalization in the U.K. Besides this FTSE 100 index, the group produces the FTSE 250, the 350, the Small Cap, and the All-Share.

The FTSE 250 companies are those next 250 largest companies after the FTSE 100. Combining the 250 and the 100 yields the 350 index. Merging the 350 and Small Cap provides the All Share Index.

London Stock Exchange launched the FTSE 100 on January 3, 1984. The companies in the index are calculated for size based on their market capitalization, or number of existing shares times the price per share. The group recalculates the indices every quarter to adjust for any of the companies in the 250 index that have moved up to the 100 index and those in the 100 group that have dropped to the 250 group.

Besides this, they have to remove companies that have been taken over or merged with others. The index must also be updated for name changes, as happened with British Gas becoming BG Group and Centrica, Midland Bank becoming HSBC, and Commercial Union Assurance becoming Aviva. Name changes, mergers, and takeovers are changed as soon as they become effective.

FTSE 100 updates its composite companies based on those which rise to a position in the top 90 largest companies on the London Stock Exchange. Those which fall to the 111th position or lower are dropped. They maintain this overlapping band so that there will not be too much change in the index in any given quarter. The group is concerned about the stability of the index and the rate of change because it forces investment companies and funds to rebalance when the benchmark 100 index changes. This is an expensive process for the large investors that the group tries to mitigate.

The 100 index and other benchmark indices are calculated up every 15 seconds throughout the trading days. The values are published in real time all day. The indices are open from 8am to 4:30pm on all weekdays that are not market holidays.

FTSE 100 is considered to be a good barometer for geopolitical and economic events throughout the world. When the major global markets soar, it does as well. When they plummet, it falls in sympathy. The largest single point drop for the 100 index happened on the day following Black Monday in the U.S. on October 20th of 1987. On this occasion, the 100 index fell 12.22% in a single trading session.

FTSE is not only a series of British stock indices. The group also produces and compiles every day more than 100,000 additional indices around the globe. Among these are the Global Equity, Italy's MIB, the China A50 and 50, the Portugal 20, and the TWSE Taiwan. In 2015 the group merged with Russell to become the FTSE Russell Group. This gave it reach into a number of American stock market indices like the Russell 2000.

Fixed Annuity

A Fixed Annuity refers to a particular form of annuity contract. Insurance companies make such contracts with individuals who are mostly saving for retirement or estate planning. Two main types of these annuities exist, variable and fixed annuities. The fixed one permits investors to add money to the account which is tax deferred. The investor furnishes a lump sum of money in exchange for which the life insurance provides a fully guaranteed and fixed interest rate at the same time as they also guarantee 100 percent of the principle invested. These annuities are often popular for their ability to offer the annuity holder (annuitant) a fully guaranteed income on a regular basis. This can be arranged as a specific number of years or for the remainder of the individual's life.

The motivation for a person to turn over a large sum of money to an insurance company for such a Fixed Annuity lies in the wish to obtain guaranteed returns while not having any original principal at risk. The second factor centers on the special tax advantages that these contracts with insurance companies enjoy. They receive many of the identical tax advantages from which life insurance policies benefit. Among these are earnings growth on a tax-deferred basis. This does not mean that taxes will not be paid, only that they will not be due until the contract becomes annuitized into monthly payouts or the earnings in the account become withdrawn.

There are a number of advantages to these types of Fixed Annuity investments that continue to draw investors to them year in and out. They offer guaranteed minimum rates, competitive yields which are fixed, guaranteed income payments, withdrawal ability, tax deferred growth, and principal safety.

The guaranteed minimum rates are nice but not forever it is important to note. These exist for an initial period only. The subsequent rates becomes adjusted utilizing a certain formula or alternatively employing whatever the prevailing yield is in the investment accounts of the insurers. Some fixed annuities will also offer an extended minimum rate guarantee as a protection in case interest rates decline in the future.

Competitive yields that are fixed come from the life insurance firm's investment portfolio which generates them. These investments mostly go into both high quality corporate bonds and U.S. government bonds. This yield is usually greater than a comparable yield on another investment which comes without risk. Many times this will be guaranteed by the insurance company for anywhere from at least one to as many as ten years.

To many annuity buyers, the guaranteed income payments are the greatest benefit to them. This feature becomes activated when the holder converts the fixed annuity into what is known as an immediate annuity. They can do this whenever they wish to provide a fully guaranteed monthly income payout that can last the remainder of the annuitant's life if they so desire.

Withdrawals are possible with these forms of Fixed Annuities. Holders can take an annual withdrawal every year that is as high as 10 percent of the value of the account. Any amounts greater than 10 percent will be penalized with a surrender charge if this occurs during the surrender period (usually ranging from seven to 12 years from contract start). Every year this surrender charge amount decreases until it eventually reaches zero. At that point withdrawals exceeding 10 percent of the account become penalty-free. There would still be the IRS tax penalty which amounts to ten percent (plus regular income taxes levied as well) on any withdrawals made before the owner reaches 59 and ½ years of age.

Principal safety is a rare commodity in these financially unstable times in the world. Annuities guarantee this, but the strength of the guarantee is only as good as the life insurance company that makes it. This is why investors should only invest their money with those life insurance firms which have at least an A or higher financial strength rating.

FTSE 100 Index

The FTSE 100 Index proves to be the trading world designation for the largest index managed by the FTSE Group out of London in the United Kingdom. FTSE is actually jointly owned by parent companies the Financial Times and the London Stock Exchange. This mash up of FT from Financial Times and SE from London Stock Exchange is how they arrive at the acronym FTSE. In general when analysts refer to the FTSE, they mean the FTSE 100 Index itself. This is actually a misnomer, since there are literally thousands of different FTSE indices the company owns and operates around the globe on numerous different national stock exchanges on every continent.

This FTSE 100 Index has been called the globe's most heavily referenced and most popular stock market index throughout the world. In practice, it represents around 80 percent of the entire market capitalization of the heavily multinational London Stock Exchange. The weighting system the FTSE company utilizes means that the bigger a corporation is, the larger a share of the index it occupies, thanks to it being a market capitalization-weighted index. This index is real time calculated all trading day long. The firm updates and publishes it continuously throughout the open market hours on an every 15 seconds basis.

Many analysts and investors rely on the FTSE 100 Index as some sort of prosperity indicator for British companies and the United Kingdom economy in general. This is actually a misnomer. It is all thanks to a significant constituency of the representative firms from the index being headquartered in other nations throughout the globe. It means that the index's daily movements do not truly reflect the strength of the British economy and corporations. Instead, the secondary index of the group, the FTSE 250 is more accurate a bell weather for British businesses and the economy. This is because a far smaller representation of international corporations populates the 250 index. It makes it a much better indicator for Great Britain generally speaking.

FTSE the company decides every quarter which are the 100 largest member companies on the LSE. Their tradition is to calculate this on the Wednesday after the first Friday of the month for March, June, September, and December, respectively. They utilize the business day close values from the night before to decide if any constituents should be replaced.

It is no exaggeration to call the FTSE 100 Index the Blue Chip index of the London Stock Exchange. These are the largest and most economically powerful and far-reaching corporations from Great Britain and around the world (ex the United States) in many cases.

The constituent members of the FTSE 100 as of time of publication were as follows: 3I Group, Associated British Foods, Admiral Group, Anglo American, Antofagasta, Ashtead Group, AstraZeneca, Aviva, Babcock International, BAE Systems, Barclays, Barratt Development, BHP Billiton, BP, British American Tobacco, British Land, BT Group, Bunzl, Burberry Group, Carnival, Centrica, Coca Cola HBC AG, Compass Group, Convatec, CRH, Croda International, DCC, Diageo, Direct Line, Easy Jet, Experian, Fresnillo, GKN, GlaxoSmithKline, Glencore, Hammerson, Hargreaves Lans, Hikma, HSBC Bank Holdings, Imperial Brands, Informa, Intercontinental Hotels, Intertek Group, International Consolidated Airlines, INTU Properties, ITV, Johnson Matthey, Kingfisher, Land Securities, Legal & General, Lloyds Group, London Stock Exchange, Marks & Spencer, Medi clinic, Merlin, Micro Focus, Mondi, William Morrison, National Grid, Next, Old Mutual, Paddy Power Betting, Pearson, Persimmon, Provident Financial, Prudential, Randgold Res., RDS A Shares, RDS B Shares, Reckitt Benison Group, RELX, Rentokil International, Rio Tinto, Rolls Royce Holdings, Royal Bank of Scotland, Royal Mail, RSA Insurance, Sage Group, J. Sainsbury, Schroders, Scottish Mort, Severn Trent, Shire Pharmaceuticals, Sky PLC, Smith & Nephew, Smiths Group, Smurfit Kap., SSE, St. James's Place, Standard Chartered, Standard Life, Taylor Wimpey, Tesco, TUI AG, Unilever, United Utilities, Vodafone Group, Whitbread, Wolseley, Worldpay Group, and WPP Group (the world's leading advertising company giant).

FTSE 250

FTSE 250 is a broad-based stock index maintained by the FTSE company. This company is much like Standard and Poor's in that they both concentrate their efforts on calculating indices. The FTSE is not made up of any stock exchange, though among its co-owners is the famed and historic London Stock Exchange (LSE). The other co-owner of the company is its namesake the Financial Times newspaper publishing empire.

Easily the best known of the FTSE indices is the FTSE 100. There are many thousands of indices owned, produced, and calculated by FTSE, but only one is the blue chip index of all British and international company and economy stocks based on the LSE. The second most important and widely cited index from the company is this FTSE 250. This one is made up of the 101st to 351st largest companies in the U.K. As these firms tend to be much more British and far less international than those making up the FTSE 100, they are gauged to be a superior measurement of how the British economy and U.K. based firms are actually performing.

The FTSE 250 index list is altered four times a year on a quarterly basis. This occurs reliably every March, June, September, and December month. The index itself is continuously calculated instantly in real time. The owner of the index publishes it every minute accordingly online and through financial news and media outlet feeds.

As of November 7, 2016, the 350 different constituent companies which comprise the FTSE 250 are as follows: 3i Infrastructure, AA, Aberdeen Asset Management, Aberforth Smaller Companies Trust, Acacia Mining, Aggreko, Aldermore Group, Alliance Trust, Allied Minds, Amec Foster Wheeler, AO World, Ascential, Ashmore Group, Assura, WS Atkins, Auto Trader Group, Aveva, Balfour Beatty, Bankers Investment Trust, Barr, A.G., BBA Aviation, Beazley Group, Bellway, Berendsen, Berkeley Group Holdings, Bank of Georgia Holdings, BH Macro, Big Yellow Group, B & M European Retail Value, Bodycote, Booker Group, Bovis Homes Group, Brewin Dolphin Holdings, British Empire Trust, Britvic, Brown N, BTG, Cairn Energy, Caledonia Investments, Capital & Counties Properties, Card Factory, Carillion, Centamin, Cineworld, City of London Investment Trust, Clarkson, Close Brothers Group, CLS Holdings, CMC Markets, Cobham, Computacenter, Countryside Properties, Countrywide, Cranswick, Crest

Nicholson, CYBG, Daejan Holdings, Dairy Crest, Debenhams, Dechra Pharmaceuticals, Derwent London, DFS, Dignity, Diploma, Domino's Pizza, Drax Group, Dunelm Group, Edinburgh Investment Trust, Electra Private Equity, Electrocomponents, Elementis, Entertainment One, Essentra, Esure, Euromoney Institutional Investor, Evraz, F&C Commercial Property Trust, Fidelity China Special Situations, Fidelity European Values, Fidessa Group, Finsbury Growth & Income Trust, FirstGroup, Fisher, James & Sons, Foreign & Colonial Investment Trust, G4S, Galliford Try, GCP Infrastructure Investments, Genesis Emerging Markets Fund, Genus, Go-Ahead Group, Grafton Group, Grainger, Great Portland Estates, Greencoat UK Wind, Greencore, Greene King, Greggs, GVC Holdings, Halfords Group, Halma, Hansteen Holdings, HarbourVest Global Private Equity, Hastings Group, Hays, Henderson Group, HICL Infrastructure Company, Hill & Smith, Hiscox, Hochschild Mining, Homeserve, Howden Joinery, Hunting, Ibstock, ICAP, IG Group Holdings, IMI, Inchcape, Indivior, Inmarsat, Intermediate Capital Group, International Personal Finance, International Public Partnerships, Investec, IP Group, Jardine Lloyd Thompson, JD Sports, John Laing Group, John Laing Infrastructure Fund, JPMorgan American Investment Trust, JPMorgan Emerging Markets Investment Trust, JPMorgan Indian Investment Trust, JRP Group, Jupiter Fund Management, Just Eat, KAZ Minerals, Keller, Kennedy Wilson Europe Real Estate, Kier Group, Ladbrokes Coral, Laird, Lancashire Holdings, LondonMetric Property, Man Group, Marshalls, Marston's, McCarthy & Stone, Meggitt, Mercantile Investment Trust, Metro Bank, Millennium & Copthorne Hotels, Mitchells & Butlers, Mitie, Moneysupermarket.com Group, Monks Investment Trust, Morgan Advanced Materials, Murray International Trust, National Express Group, NB Global, NCC Group, NMC Health, Ocado Group, OneSavings Bank, P2P Global Investments, PageGroup, Paragon Group of Companies, PayPoint, Paysafe, Pennon Group, Perpetual Income & Growth Investment Trust, Personal Assets Trust, Petra Diamonds, Petrofac, Pets at Home, Phoenix Group Holdings, Playtech, Polar Capital Technology Trust, Polypipe, PZ Cussons, QinetiQ, Rank Group, Rathbone Brothers, Redefine International, Redrow, Regus, Renewables Infrastructure Group, Renishaw, Rentokil Initial, Restaurant Group, Rightmove, RIT Capital Partners, Riverstone Energy, Rotork, RPC Group, Safestore, Saga, Savills, Scottish Investment Trust, Scottish Mortgage Investment Trust, Segro, Senior, Serco, Shaftesbury, Shawbrook Bank, SIG plc, Smith (DS), Smurfit Kappa Group, Softcat, Sophos, Spectris, Spirax-Sarco Engineering, Spire Healthcare, Sports Direct, SSP

Group, Stagecoach Group, St. Modwen Properties, SuperGroup, SVG Capital, Synthomer, TalkTalk Group, Tate & Lyle, Ted Baker, Telecom Plus, Temple Bar Investment Trust, Templeton Emerging Markets Investment Trust, Thomas Cook Group, Tritax Big Box REIT, TR Property Investment Trust (two listings, both ordinary & sigma shares), Tullett Prebon, Tullow Oil, UBM, UDG Healthcare, UK Commercial Property Trust, Ultra Electronics Holdings, Unite Group, Vectura Group, Vedanta Resources, Vesuvius, Victrex, Virgin Money, Weir Group, Wetherspoon (J D), W H Smith, William Hill, Witan Investment Trust, Wizz Air, Woodford Patient Capital Trust, Wood Group, Workspace Group, Worldwide Healthcare Trust, and Zoopla.

Futures Exchange

A futures exchange refers to a central clearing marketplace that allows for futures contracts as well as options on such futures contracts to be traded. Thanks to the rapid increase in electronic trading of futures, this term also finds use regarding futures trading activities directly.

There are the two most important futures exchanges in the world today. The biggest in the United States is the Chicago Mercantile Exchange, or CME. This one became established in the last years of the 1890s. In the early days, the only futures contracts available were agricultural products' futures.

This changed rapidly in the 1970s. Currency futures appeared on the major currency pairs after the breakdown of the Breton Woods Agreement. The futures exchanges of today are massive by comparison. They allow for investors to hedge all sorts of financial products and commodities. These range from stock indices and individual stocks to energies, precious and base metals, soft commodities such as orange juice and soybeans, interest rate products, and even credit default swaps.

In today's futures exchange, it is hedging financial instruments and products which create the significant majority of activity in futures markets. Today the futures exchange markets carry an important responsibility for global financial system operations, efficient functioning, and activity. The international nature of this global futures exchange has given rise to the world's first truly international futures market, the ICE Intercontinental Exchange.

ICE is massive and important in not only futures markets. They own and operate 12 different exchanges around the world, including NYSE EuroNext, which controls the famed and venerable New York Stock Exchange and EuroNext exchange (owning the Paris and Dutch stock exchanges, among others). In Europe, this is a serious rival to the historic LSE London Stock Exchange and continental powerhouse the German Deutsche Bourse. The ICE today counts 12,000 listed futures contracts as well as securities. It trades 5.2 million futures contracts every day, as well as $1.8 billion in cash equities every day.

In energies, the Intercontinental Exchange Futures commands almost half of all the traded crude and refined oil futures contracts volume for the entire planet. It is also the location of the most highly liquid market for the European interest rates short term contracts. It controls a wide variety of global benchmarks in agriculture, energies, foreign exchange, and equity indices.

ICE only launched its international futures exchange back in 2000 with the advent of their electronic trading platform. This makes it among the newer futures exchanges in the world, and yet it is a dominant international player still. Their high tech-powered rise increased the access to and transparency of the Over the Counter traded energy markets as well as the new global futures markets exchange they opened shortly thereafter. It was 2001 when they expanded to energy futures with their acquisition of the International Petroleum Exchange.

In 2002, ICE expanded heavily into Europe by opening up their ICE Clear Europe. This represented the first new clearing house in the United Kingdom in a full century. By 2007, the Intercontinental Exchange had cemented its global position in energy trade by acquiring both the NYBOT New York Board of Trade and the Canadian-based Winnipeg Commodity Exchange.

The end result today is an entire ecosystem made up of futures and equities markets, clearing houses throughout the world, listing and data centers and services, and technology-driven solutions which together work to create a full, free, and transparent accessibility to the worldwide futures, energy, derivatives, and capital markets.

Between ICE Futures U.S.'s operations and endeavors within the United States, the futures exchange is enabling and empowering markets which allow for an effective risk management throughout the world economy. Their product offerings and solutions encompass a diverse and broad variety of futures contracts. These span internationally traded equity indexes and futures; credit derivative futures; FX futures; North American oil, power, and natural gas futures; and soft commodities and agriculture futures including sugar, cotton, coffee, and cocoa.

General Obligation Bonds

General Obligation Bonds are municipal bonds which are reinforced by the full taxing powers and overall credit worthiness of the jurisdiction which issues them instead of a certain revenue stream from the associated specific project. These special general types of bonds are floated by municipalities under the belief that the jurisdiction will have the resources in the future to pay back all of its debts via general taxation or incoming revenue from other projects. With these GO bonds, there is no collateral from other underlying assets of the issuer.

What makes these general obligation bonds so appealing to investors even though they have no underlying security behind them is that the issuing government agency has promised to utilize every available resource, including tax revenues, in order to pay back the bond holders. Such pledges from local governments can include a promise to assess special property taxes so that the government entity is able to meet its obligations to the bond holders. As an example, property owners have skin in the game because of their local area property holdings and any unpaid property tax obligations.

Credit ratings agencies will analyze and rate the pledges of general obligations according to the strength of their credit qualities. They then assign them generally high investment graded ratings. When said property owners are incapable of paying in their fare share of property taxes according to the final due date, the government is permitted legally to raise the effective rates of property taxes in order to compensate for any delinquencies. On these required due dates, a general obligation bond pledge will mandate that the local government entity has to pay its owed debt using the resources which are available.

These general obligation bonds are also useful for the local area governments to be able to raise sufficient funds for needed projects which will build up revenue streams for projects including bridges and roads, equipment, and parks. Such bonds are generally utilized to pay for government infrastructure projects which will serve the general good of the public at large.

It is actually the relevant state laws which set the stage for what local governments are allowed to issue in the forms of these general obligation bonds. They can be unlimited tax obligation pledges or limited tax obligation promises to repay. Unlimited tax obligations are much like the limited tax promises. The principal difference pertains to the local government being required to raise property tax rates to levels that will service the debts, even as high as 100%, in order to cover other taxpayer delinquencies. It is up to the local residents to agree in advance to property tax increases which are needed to repay the bonds.

Alternatively the limited tax obligation pledges request that the local government issuing the bonds will increase the property taxes as needed in order to cover the debt service obligations. There is a statutory limit that provides boundaries for these. Governments are able to employ a portion of the property taxes which are already levied, increase existing property tax rates to a level that will service the debt payments, or utilize an alternative revenue stream in order to pay the debts as required by the terms of the general obligation bonds.

Such general obligation bonds are usually considered to be the safest form of municipal bonds because they are backed up by the ability of the issuer to tax. There are also other reasons that give them their aura of perceived safety. Companies may go bankrupt every day of the year, but municipalities can not.

They have therefore a far greater motivation to maintain their precious credit ratings since they can not simply go bankrupt and disappear into oblivion. They will also have to return to the bond markets periodically at other points in the future so that they can fund still more projects for their constituents. Besides this, the state laws generally detail the precise conditions under which the issuing municipalities are able to issue such general obligation bonds, as well as the kind of security they are able to utilize.

Hedge Fund

A hedge fund is an investment fund which are commonly only open to a specific group of investors. These investors pay a large performance fee each year, commonly a certain percent of their funds under management, to the manager of the hedge fund. Hedge funds are very minimally regulated and are therefore are able to participate in a wide array of investments and investment strategies.

Literally every single hedge fund pursues its own strategy of investing that will establish the kinds of investments that it seeks. Hedge funds commonly go for a wide range of investments in which they may buy or sell short shares and positions. Stocks, commodities, and bonds are some of these asset classes with which they work.

As you would anticipate from the name, hedge funds typically try to offset some of the risks in their portfolios by employing a number of risk hedging strategies. These mostly revolve around the use of derivatives, or financial instruments with values that depend on anticipated price movements in the future of an asset to which they are linked, as well as short selling investments.

Most countries only allow certain types of wealthy and professional investors to open a hedge fund account. Regulators may not heavily oversee the activities of hedge funds, but they do govern who is allowed to participate. As a result, traditional investment funds' rules and regulations mostly do not apply to hedge funds.

Actual net asset values of hedge funds often tally into the many billions of dollars. The funds' gross assets held commonly prove to be massively higher as a result of their using leverage on their money invested. In particular niche markets like distressed debt, high yield ratings, and derivatives trading, hedge funds are the dominant players.

Investors get involved in hedge funds in search of higher than normal market returns. When times are good, many hedge funds yield even twenty percent annual investment returns. The nature of their hedging strategies is supposed to protect them from terrible losses, such as were seen in the financial crisis from 2007-2010.

The hedge fund industry is opaque and difficult to measure accurately. This is partially as a result of the significant expansion of the industry, as well as an inconsistent definition of what makes a hedge fund. Prior to the peak of hedge funds in the summer of 2008, it is believed that hedge funds might have overseen as much as two and a half trillion dollars. The credit crunch hit many hedge funds particularly hard, and their assets under management have declined sharply as a result of both losses, as well as requests for withdrawals by investors. In 2010, it is believed that hedge funds once again represent in excess of two trillion dollars in assets under management.

The largest hedge funds in the world are JP Morgan Chase, with over $53 billion under management; Bridgewater Associates, having more than $43 billion in assets under management; Paulson and Company, with more than $32 billion in assets; Brevan Howard that has greater than $27 billion in assets; and Soros Fund Management, which boasts around $27 billion in assets under management.

High Yield Bonds

High Yield Bonds turn out to be bonds that possess a lower credit rating and higher yield than those corporate, municipal, and sovereign government bonds which are of investment grade. Thanks to the greater risk of them defaulting, such bonds yield a higher return than the bonds which are qualified investment grade issues. Those companies that issue high yielding debt are usually capital intensive companies and startup firms that already possess higher debt ratios. Investors often refer to such bonds as junk bonds.

The two principal corporate rating credit agencies determine the breakdown of what qualifies as a High Yield Bond and what does not. When Moody's rates a bond with lower than a "Baa" rating, or Standard and Poor's (S&P) rates then with an under "BBB" rating, then they become known as junk bonds. At the same time, all of those bonds which enjoy higher ratings than these (or the same rating at least) investors will consider to be investment grade. There are credit ratings that cover such categories as presently in default, or "D." Those kinds of bonds holding "C" ratings and below also have high probabilities for defaulting. In order to compensate the investors who take them on for the significant risks they run of not receiving either their original principal back or accrued interest payments by the maturity date, the yields must be offered at extremely high interest rates.

Despite the negative label of "junk bond," these High Yield Bonds remain popular and heavily bought by global investors. The majority of these investors choose to diversify for safety sake by utilizing either a junk bond ETF exchange traded fund or a High Yield Bonds mutual fund. The spread between the yields on the higher yielding and investment grade types of bonds constantly fluctuates on the markets. The at the time condition of the global and national economies impacts this. Industry-specific and individual corporate events also play a part in the differences between the various kinds of bonds' interest rates.

In general though, High Yield Bonds' investors can count on receiving a good 150 to 300 basis points more in yield as measured against the investment quality bonds in any particular time frame. This is why mutual funds and ETFs make imminent sense as an effective means of gaining exposure to the greater yields without taking on the unnecessary risk of a single issuer's bonds defaulting and costing the investors all or most of their original investing principal.

In the last few years, various central bankers throughout the globe have decided to inject enormous amounts of liquidity into their individual economies so that credit will remain cheaply and easily available. This includes the European Central Bank, the U.S. Federal Reserve, and the Bank of Japan. It has created the side effect of causing borrowing costs to drop and lenders to experience significantly lower returns.

By February of 2016, an incredible $9 trillion in sovereign government debt bonds provided yields of only from zero percent to one percent. Seven trillion of the sovereign bonds delivered negative real yields once adjusted for anticipated levels of inflation. It means that holding such bonds cost investors money, or provided them a real losing return.

In typical economic environments, this would drive intelligent investors to competing markets that provide better return rates. Higher yield bond markets have stayed volatile though. Distressed debts which pay minimally a yield higher than 1,000 basis points greater than a comparably maturing Treasury bond were notably affected. Energy company high yielding debt bond prices collapsed by approximately 20 percent in 2015 as a consequence of the problems in the energy sector which resulted from plummeting energy prices.

High Yield Preferred Stocks

Preferred stocks are a special type of stocks that many companies issue. These types of stocks provide investors with a different level of ownership in a given company. A preferred stock holder obtains a higher priority on the earnings and assets of a company than a common stock holder would enjoy. These preferred stocks also pay a higher dividend that has to be given out before any dividends can be paid to the common stock holders.

As such, they represent a hybrid type of security on the stock markets. They are like common stocks in that they are bought and sold as stocks and represent ownership in a company. These stocks can also trade up and down in price like a common stock. Unlike a common stock, they do not come with any rights to vote for a company board of directors or items on a company ballot at the annual meeting.

They are also like bonds in that they pay a higher dividend that must be paid out unless the company lacks the earnings to pay these holders. In this way preferred stocks have elements of bonds with their fixed rate of dividends. Every preferred stock comes with its own unique details that are set when the company issues the stock.

Preferred stocks are often higher yielding issues. They are most commonly issued by companies that are in industries such as financials, real estate investment trusts, utilities, industrials, and conglomerates. Despite this higher yield that makes them like bonds, they can be traded on the major stock exchanges. They are typically found on exchanges including the NASDAQ and the New York Stock Exchange.

As preferred stocks are a type of equity legally, they show up as equity on any company balance sheet. Both common and preferred stock holders are owners in the company. There are several advantages to preferred stocks that investors like about them.

In the past, individual retail investors were less aware of preferred stocks, but this is changing. Part of the reason they have gained in popularity surrounds market volatility. As common stocks have seen wild price swings in recent years, investors have been looking for more stable instruments in which they can invest.

Preferred stocks fit this need as they tend to be more stable in price than do common stocks. With more baby boomers looking for investments that provide higher yields, this has brought preferred stocks into the spotlight. The retirees gain the advantage of better yields and the opportunity for the price to increase in the issues as well.

Preferred stocks are not new. They have existed from the time when modern day investing began. Institutional investors have known about and invested in them for many decades. Many individual investors did not because they lacked the information they required to select and trade them.

In the past, individuals did not have any lists of preferred stocks from which to pick. The information available was difficult to come up with before the Internet made this kind of information much more readily available. Now there are tools smaller individual investors can find that provide calendar searches for ex-dividend dates.

There are also screening filters that allow individuals to narrow down their search for the best high yielding dividend preferred stocks. Preferred stocks represent another way to diversify an investor's portfolio and earn higher yields on dividends at the same time.

Index Funds

Index funds are typically exchange traded funds or mutual funds. Their goal is to reproduce the actual movements of an underlying index for a particular financial market. They do this no matter what is happening in the overall stock markets.

There are several means of tracking such an index. One way of doing this is by purchasing and holding all of the index securities to the same proportion as they are represented in the index. Another way of accomplishing this is by doing a statistical sample of the market and then acquiring securities that are representative of it. A great number of the index funds are based on a computer model that accepts little to no input from people in its decision making of the securities bought and sold. This qualifies as a type of passive management when the index fund is run this way.

These index funds do not have active management. This allows them to benefit from possessing lesser fees and taxes in their accounts that are taxable. The low fees that are charged do come off of the investment returns that are otherwise mostly matching those of the index. Besides this, exactly matching an index is not possible since the sampling and mirroring models of this index will never be one hundred percent right. Such variances between an index performance and that of the fund are referred to as the tracking error, or more conversationally as a jitter.

A wide variety of index funds exist for you to choose from these days. They are offered by a number of different investment managers as well. Among the more typically seen indices are the FTSE 100, the S&P 500, and the Nikkei 225. Other indexes have been created that are so called research indexes for creating asset pricing models. Kenneth French and Eugene Fama created one known as the Three Factor Model. This Fama-French three factor model is actually utilized by Dimensional Fund Advisers to come up with their various index funds. Other, newer indexes have been created that are known as fundamentally based indexes. These find their basis in factors like earnings, dividends, sales, and book values of companies.

The underlying concept for developing index funds comes from the EMH, or efficient market hypothesis. This hypothesis claims that because stock analysts and fund managers are always searching for stocks that will do better than the whole market, this efficient competition among them translates to current information on a company's affairs being swiftly factored into the price of the stock. Because of this, it is generally accepted that knowing which stocks will do better than the over all market in advance is exceedingly hard. Developing a market index then makes sense as the inefficiencies and risks inherent in picking out individual stocks can be simply eliminated through purchasing the index fund itself.

Institutional Investor

Institutional investors turn out to be organizations or occasionally individuals which buy and sell securities in huge enough quantities and currency totals. They benefit from lower fees and commissions as well as special treatment from the market makers.

These large and powerful deep pocketed investors experience fewer regulations from the regulatory agencies as well since they naturally assume that they have a larger knowledge base and are sophisticated enough to protect themselves in their investing strategies. There are many different kinds of investors who qualify as institutional investors. Some of them are life insurance firms and pension funds.

These entities derive their money from a variety of sources, but in all cases they pool the funds in order to buy and sell real estate, stock and bond securities, and other alternative types of investment classes such as loans, commodities, precious metals, and artwork.

There are many different kinds of institutional investors such as hedge funds, pension funds, insurance companies, sovereign wealth funds, commercial banks, investment advisors, Real Estate Investment Trusts, mutual funds, and university endowments. Other operating firms that choose to invest their extra capital in such asset classes are also covered by the term. Some institutional investors are activist. This means that they may interfere with the internal workings and governance of the firm by using their substantial voting rights in the companies in which they own larger stakes to influence corporate decisions, investments, and behavior.

Institutional investors act as intermediaries between smaller retail investors and corporations. They are also significant sources of critical capital for the financial markets. Since they pool together their member investment dollars or Euros, these larger and more powerful investors effectively lessen the cost of capital to entrepreneurs at the same time as the efficiently diversify their clients' portfolios. Since they can impact the behavior of companies as well, this helps to reduce agency costs.

Institutional investors have several significant and game changing advantages over smaller, weaker retail investors. They possess enormous resources to invest as well as specialty knowledge that pertains to a variety of different investment options. Many of these choices are not even available to traditional retail investors at all. They also have longer term investing horizons as they are not limited to accumulation and distribution requirements of individual investors who will want to transition to retirement at some point.

Such institutions turn out to be the biggest movers and shakers within both supply and demand segments in the securities markets. This means that they transact the overwhelming majority of all trades on the major stock and bond market exchanges. Their choices and actions substantially impact the prices and bid/asks of most securities on the various markets.

This has led a number of retail investors to attempt to level the proverbial playing field of investing by researching the various filings of holdings the institutions make with the SEC Securities and Exchange Commission to learn what different securities they ought to invest in for their own individual portfolios and trades.

Some of these institutional investors are critically important in specific types of countries. For example, those countries which are oil rich and exporting nations generally contain one or more massive sovereign wealth funds which possess a lion's share of the investable wealth of the nation. These are usually government controlled and administered institutional funds and investors.

They can amass even hundreds of billions of investable dollars, as have the Norwegian, Abu Dhabi, Saudi Arabian, Qatari, and Kuwaiti funds. In developed nations, it is the pension funds and insurance companies which control a substantial portion of the excess and readily deployable and investable capital.

Internal Rate of Return (IRR)

The IRR is the acronym for internal rate of return. This IRR proves to be the capital budget rate of return that is utilized in order to determine and compare and contrast various investments' profitability. It is sometimes known as the discounted cash flow rate of return alternatively, or even the ROR, or rate of return. Where banks are concerned, the IRR is also known as the effective interest rate. The word internal is used to specify that such calculation does not involve facts that are part of the external environment, such as inflation or the interest rate.

More precisely, the internal rate of return for any investment proves to be the interest rate level where the negative cash flow, or net present value of costs, from the investment is equal to the positive cash flow, or net present value of benefits, for the investment. In other words, this IRR will yield a discount rate that causes the net current values of both positive and negative cash flows of a specific investment to cancel out at zero.

These Internal Rates of Return are generally utilized to consider projects and investments and their ultimate desirability. Naturally, a project will be more appealing to engage in or purchase if it comes with a greater internal rate of return. Given a number of projects from which to choose, and assuming that all project benefits prove to be the same generally, the project that contains the greatest Internal Rate of Return will be considered the most attractive. It should be selected with the highest priority of being pursued first.

The assumed theory for companies is that they will be interested in eventually pursuing any investment or project that comes with an IRR that is greater than the expense of the money put into the project as capital. The number of projects or investments that can be run at a time are limited in the real world though. A firm may have a restricted capability of overseeing a large number of projects at once, or they may lack the necessary funds to engage in all of them at a time.

The internal rate of return is actually a number expressed as a percent. It details the yield, efficacy, and efficiency of a given investment or project. This should not be confused with the net present value that instead tells the particular investment's actual value.

In general, a given investment or project is deemed to be worthwhile assuming that its internal rate of return proves to be higher than either the expense of the capital involved, or alternatively, than a pre set minimally accepted rate of return. For companies that possess share holders, the minimum IRR is always a factor of the investment capital's cost. This is easily decided by ascertaining the cost of capital, which is risk adjusted, for alternative types of investments. In this way, share holders will approve of a project or investment, so long as its Internal Rate of Return is greater than the cost of the capital to be used and this project or investment creates economic value that is viable for the company in question.

Investment Management

Investment Management proves to be a general term which most often relates to purchasing and selling investments inside of a portfolio. It might also be utilized to cover budgeting and banking tasks and tax management. Most of the time, the phrase pertains to managing portfolios and trading securities to reach a particular set of investment goals or objectives.

Analysts and economists also call Investment Management by the names of money management, private banking, or even portfolio management. This includes the professional money management of various assets and financial instruments. Among these are equities, bonds, real estate, and other types of securities such as gold, derivatives, and mortgage-backed securities. Successful and well-rounded management of investments works to achieve particular investment objectives for the good of the underlying investors. Such investors are not necessarily individuals, or private investors. They are often family investment offices as well as institutional investors. Among the various deep-pocketed institutional investors are governments, pension funds, sovereign wealth funds, insurance companies, and educational foundations.

The services of Investment Managers cover many functions. These include analysis of financial statements and assets, proper asset allocation and diversification, investment instruments and stocks selection, financial plan implementation, estate planning, and maintenance of existing investments in the portfolios. An entire industry has grown up around these needs for wealthy clients and investors. This is called the Investment Management industry.

For those who feel led to start an Investment Management firm, there are many important and sensitive tasks that must be successfully accomplished. This starts with hiring professional money managers. It extends to performing research on types of asset classes and particular investments. Marketing, dealing, settling, and internal auditing are all core functions on the administration side of the business. Finally, this type of firm will have to prepare regular reports and statements for the various clientele.

This means that it requires much more than simply hiring an effective asset gathering marketing team and a highly qualified and results-driven money management staff to manage the daily flow of investing. Owners of these firms must also handle the various jurisdictional regulatory and legislative environments, carefully monitor the business' cash flow, stay on top of the internal controls and all systems, and accurately record and track all fund values and any transactions performed.

This means that Investment Management firms have a certain set of stressful problems that they deal with routinely. This is the trade off for what can be substantial and highly lucrative rewards. First of all, investment management firms are highly dependent for their income on the performance of the various asset markets. In other words, the firm's profits will often come down to the progress of the markets. When asset prices suffer a substantial decline, this will undoubtedly lead to the management firm's revenues dropping off. This is particularly the case when the fall in prices is higher than the investment basis cost of the company.

There are also issues of client expectation management. When times in the markets are hard and lean, clients can become agitated, impatient, and even angry. Even fund performance which is above industry average may not be good enough to keep the clients satisfied with their portfolios' progress. This is the reason it is critical for any investment management company to attract and retain highly successful money managers. The problem with this is that top talent is costly and hard to keep loyal when the competition is always hungry for and eager to steal effective money managers.

For clients who are seriously contemplating a particular Investment Management firm, it is a common mistake to single out only the performance of one particular investment manager on staff. Instead the all-around total performance of the investment firm is what matters. This is why a successful investment company will have to retain expensive and performance-generating investment managers in order for their clientele to be willing to trust in the firm to manage their money.

Investment Trusts

An investment trust represent a type of collective investment pool generally utilized in Great Britain. These closed end funds are established as public limited companies within the United Kingdom primarily. Analysts have stated that the British investment trust was a forerunner of the American-promoted investment company.

In truth the name is somewhat of a misnomer. These investment trusts are not actually legal trust entities whatsoever. Instead they are a legal company or even individual. The reason this is important is because of the fiduciary responsibilities that trustees owe their membership.

When the fund is first established, a pool of all investors' funds becomes created. The investors then received a set amount of the fixed total number of shares that the trust floats on the launch date. Boards usually hand over the responsibility of the fund management into the care of a professional fund manager. This manager will then invest the fund's money into a vast range of individual shares of different corporations. This provides the fund investors with a massive diversification into a number of different companies that they could not possibly afford to do using their own limited resources.

These investment trusts may not have any employees, but instead count just a board of directors which is made up of exclusively non-executive directors. This has begun to change over the last few years as competition in the form of other funds emerged. Thanks to commercial property trusts and private equity groups utilizing the investment trust structure for holding vehicles, the structure of the staff and boards has changed in some cases.

Shares of investment trusts trade on various stock exchanges as do shares of typical publicly held corporations. What makes the value of these shares of the investment trusts interesting is that the offered price per share is not always the same as what the underlying share value should be based on the portfolio which the trust holds. When this happens, analysts say that the trust itself trades for a discount or a premium to its actual NAV net asset value.

This sector of the investment trust experienced significant trouble in the years from 2000 through 2003. This was because there was no set compensation plan for the industry. They then came up with guidelines for compensation packages and this cleared up many of the issues overshadowing the space.

One should not confuse investment trusts and unit (investment) trusts. There are some key differences between the two. The manager of an investment trust has the carte blanche legal ability to borrow funds in order to buy shares in company stocks. The managers of unit trusts (which are open ended funds) may not do this without first having a process for risk management established that makes rules on the ways the leverage will be considered and permitted. Such gearing can boost gains earned on investments yet also dramatically expands the risk to investors.

These investment trusts have a history going back around 150 years. The first one established was the 1868 founded Foreign & Colonial Investment Trust. Its stated goal was to "give the investor of moderate means the same advantages as the large capitalists in diminishing the risk of spreading the investment over a number of stocks."

The investment trust is classified in a breakdown by similar characteristics. This permits prospective investors to compare and contrast the various trusts within a certain category more effectively. The trusts are also further broken down according to the kinds of shares they issue. Traditional investment trusts possess only the single class of ordinary shares and enjoy an unending investment vehicle lifespan.

With the rival Splits, or Split Capital Investment Trusts, the structure proves to be more complex. They issues several varying share classes so that investors can match the shares up with their own investment objectives. The majority of such Splits begin with a preset investment life span that the fund determines when it launches. They call this the wind up date. The average wind up date of such a Split Capital Investment Trust occurs between five and ten years from the fund establishment.

Junk Bonds

Junk bonds are almost the same as regular bonds with an important difference. They are lower rated for credit worthiness. This is why in order to understand junk bonds, individuals first must comprehend the basics of traditional bonds.

Like traditional bonds, junk bonds are promises from organizations or companies to pay back the holder the amount of money which they borrow. This amount is known as the principal. Terms of such bonds involve several elements. The maturity date is the time when the borrower will repay the bond holder. There will also be an interest rate that the bond holder receives, or a coupon. Junk bonds are unlike those traditional ones because the credit quality of the issuing organization is lower.

Every kind of bond is rated according to its credit quality. Bonds can all be categorized in one of two types. Investment grade bonds possess medium to low risk. Their credit ratings are commonly in the range of from AAA to BBB. The downside to these bonds is that they do not provide much in the way of interest returns. Their advantage is that they have significantly lower chances of the borrower being unable to make interest payments.

Junk bonds on the other hand offer higher interest yields to their bond holders. Issuers do this because they do not have any other way to finance their needs. With a lower credit rating, they can not borrow capital at a more favorable price. The ratings on such junk bonds are often BB or less from Standard & Poor's or Ba or less by Moody's rating agency. Bond ratings such as these can be considered like a report card for the credit rating of the company in question. Riskier firms receive lower ratings while safe blue-chip companies earn higher ratings.

Junk bonds typically pay an average yield that is from 4% to 6% higher than U.S. Treasury yields. These types of bonds are placed into one of two categories. These are fallen angels and rising stars. Fallen angels bonds used to be considered at an investment grade. They were cut to junk bond level as the company that issued them saw its credit quality decline.

Rising stars are the opposites of fallen angels. This means the rating of the bond has risen. As the underlying issuer's credit quality improves, so does the rating of the bond. Rising stars are often still considered to be junk bonds. They are on track to rise to investment quality.

Junk bonds are risky for more reasons than the chances of not receiving one or more interest payments. There is the possibility of not receiving the original principal back. This type of investing also needs a great amount of skills in analyzing data like special credit. Because of these risk factors and specialized skills that are needed, institutional investors massively dominate the market.

A better way for individuals to become involved with junk bonds is through high yield bond funds. Professionals research and manage the holdings of these funds. The risks associated with a single bond defaulting are greatly reduced. They do this by diversifying into a variety of companies and types of bonds. High yield bond funds often require investors to stay invested for minimally a year or two.

When the yield of junk bonds declines below the typical 4% to 6% spread above Treasuries, investors should be careful. The risk does not become less in these cases. It is that the returns no longer justify the dangers in the junk bonds. Investors also should carefully consider the junk bond default rates. These can be tracked for free on Moody's website.

Lease

Leases are contracts made between an owner, or lessor, and a user, or lesee, covering the utilization of an asset. Leases can pertain to business or real estate. There are a variety of different types of leases that vary with the property in question being leased.

Tangible property and assets are leased under rental agreements. Intangible property leases are much like a license, only they have differing provisions. The utilization of a computer program or a cell phone service's radio frequency are two example of such an intangible lease.

A gross lease is another type of lease. In a gross lease, a tenant actually gives a certain defined dollar amount in rent. The landlord is then responsible for any and all property expenses that are routinely necessary in owning the asset. This includes everything from washing machines to lawnmowers.

You also encounter leases that are cancelable. Cancelable leases can be ended at the discretion of the end user or lessor. Other leases are non cancelable and may not be ended ahead of schedule. In daily conversation, a lease denotes a lease that can not be broken, while a rental agreement often can be canceled.

A lease contract typically lays out particular provisions concerning both rights and obligations of the lessor and the lessee. Otherwise, a local law code's provisions will apply. When the holder of the lease, also known as the tenant, pays the arranged fee to the owner of the property, the tenant gains exclusive use and possession of the property that is leased to the point that the owner and any other individuals may not utilize it without the tenant's specific invitation. By far the most typical type of hard property lease proves to be the residential types of rental agreements made between landlords and their tenants. This type of relationship that the two parties establish is also known as a tenancy. The tenant's right to possess the property is many times referred to as the leasehold interest. These leases may exist for pre arranged amounts of time, known as a lease term. In many cases though, they can be terminated in advance, although this does depend on the particular lease's terms and conditions.

Licenses are similar to leases, but not the same thing. The main difference between the two lies in the nature of the ongoing payments and termination. When keeping the property is only accomplished by making regular payments, and can not be terminated unless the money is not paid or some form of misconduct is discovered, then the agreement is a lease. One time uses of or entrances to property are licenses. The defining difference between the two proves to be that leases require routine payments in their term and come with a particular date of ending.

Margin Call

Margin Call refers to a demand from a broker that the account holding investor (who is utilizing margin) deposit additional funds or securities in order to restore the margin account to a minimum preset maintenance margin level. This could occur with a stock, futures, or commodities margin account. Such margin calls happen as the account value falls to a ratio which that specific brokerage deems unacceptable. Many brokerage houses use their own unique formulas to determine the amount at which they will issue such a call for more funds or securities.

Investors get into this unpleasant position when one or many of their securities they have purchased (utilizing money they borrowed from the brokerage) drops to a specified value point. That is when the call goes out from the broker for more money to restore the account to an acceptable minimum value. Investors will have two choices. They could comply with the request for additional funds and make an urgent deposit. Otherwise, they could sell off some or all of the positions in the account to reduce the need for minimum margin maintenance or raise the account equity position. The third choice of completely disregarding or ignoring the margin call would result in the broker force-selling positions to reduce this maintenance amount required.

Margin calls would not be necessary at all if investors did not buy securities, futures, or commodities with a combination of their own cash plus money they borrow off of the broker. This is why many experts recommend not utilizing such margin accounts unless an investor is a both seasoned and experienced trader.

Investors have equity in these margin-purchased investments. This amount equals the securities market value less the funds they originally borrowed to complete the purchase in the first place. If and when this equity of the account holder drops to lower than the brokerage-set percentage requirement of maintenance margin, then such a margin call becomes issued. Such maintenance margins do vary somewhat significantly from one broker to the next.

The constant is the Federal minimum maintenance margin requirements. These are set at a lowest common requirement of 25 percent, regardless of who the responsible broker is. The brokers can choose to utilize a higher margin maintenance level than this amount, but they can not ever reduce their own limit to less than the 25 percent set by the Feds. Brokers can decide to change their maintenance level higher or lower than their present set one with little to no advance warning or notice, so long as they do not drop it below the government-mandated minimum amount. Raising their margin maintenance requirements may also result in creating a margin call.

Looking at a tangible example helps to clarify the concept and make it more understandable. Investors might purchase $50,000 worth of stocks via a combination of $25,000 of their own funds and through borrowing the balance $25,000 off of the brokerage firm. Assume that this particular broker chooses to utilize the government-set minimum of 25 percent maintenance margin. The investor has no choice but to honor this.

When the investors open the trade, at that point the equity positions of the investments prove to be $25,000 (or $50,000 minus the $25,000 borrowed). This makes the investor equity percentage an even 50 percent (using the $25,000 equity divided by the $50,000 original securities market value). This is twice the required minimum 25 percent margin maintenance.

Yet a week later, our investors suffer a drastic decline in the value of their securities, which precipitously drop to $30,000. The investors' equity is now down to a mere $5,000 (or $30,000 minus the $25,000 borrowed). Yet the brokerage (and government regulations which are the same in this scenario) requires that they keep a minimally $7,500 worth of equity for the account to remain margin-eligible (which is 25 percent of the borrowed amount of $30,000).

It means that there is presently a $2,500 deficit ($7,500 requirement minus the $5,000 actual market value). The broker will then issue a margin call for $2,500 in additional cash to be deposited immediately. Should the investors refuse or take their time, then the broker is legally bound and permitted to sell off some of the securities to reach the minimum $7,500 in account equity value.

Money Market Funds

Money market funds are investment vehicles with a unique objective of keeping a consistent NAV net asset value of $1 each share while they provide interest for their investing share holders. To accomplish this, the portfolio of a money market fund is made up of securities that are short term in nature with maturities which are under a year. These securities typically are liquid debt and money instruments that are of the highest quality. Investors can easily buy money market fund shares by going through banks, brokerage firms, or mutual funds directly.

The ultimate goal of these money market funds is to give their investors a safe haven investment for assets which are both readily accessible and equivalent to cash. In essence they are mutual funds. Among their most common characteristics are that they offer low returns and provide low risk as an investment.

Because these funds offer comparatively lower returns than many other investments, financial advisors recommend that investors not remain in these vehicles as a long term selection. Their returns will not provide sufficient appreciation on capital in order to achieve the investors' objectives over a longer time frame. Employer provided retirement plans will often sweep employees' unallocated dollars into these funds until they give orders as to where to invest them specifically.

The pros to money market funds can be significant. They offer more than simply high liquidity and lower risk. A number of investors find them appealing because there are not any fund entrance or exit fees (or loads) as with many mutual funds. A variety of them will offer investors gains which have tax advantages. These come from investments they make in state and federally tax exempt municipal securities. Other investments which these funds could hold include T-bills and other shorter time frame government debt issues, corporate commercial paper, and CDs certificates of deposit.

There are also some downsides to money market funds besides their low returns. Though they are supposed to be stable and consistent in their values, they are not insured by the FDIC Federal Deposit Insurance Corporation. This means that in the rare cases where such funds break the buck, investors can suffer losses of principal. Competing investments like CDs, savings accounts, and money market deposits accounts provide similar returns but do offer this government backed guarantee of principal. This does not stop investors from regarding money market funds as extremely safe. The funds are carefully regulated by the Investment Company Act of 1940.

The government changed the rules on such money market funds regarding their net asset values and in what they could invest in 2014. After that year, the funds were not permitted to set their NAV permanently at $1 any longer. They did this because of the three times in the history of such funds where the $1 share price had been broken (as of 2016). It had created "bank runs" on the assets of the money market funds in 2008 when it occurred most recently in the Financial Crisis.

The American SEC Securities and Exchange Commission decided to prevent this from happening again by changing the fund management rules to provide them with more resilience and better stability. Such new restrictions more strictly limited the assets these funds were allowed to hold. The SEC also introduced triggers that would suspend redemptions and charge liquidity fees to prevent chaos in the markets. The fund managers had to start utilizing a floating NAV which created risk where it was not perceived to exist previously. Individual investors were not impacted by the floating NAV share rule since the funds are designated as retail funds and are exempt from this rule.

Mortgage Backed Obligations (MBO)

Mortgage Backed Obligations are also called mortgage backed securities, or MBS. These are real estate-based financial instruments. They represent an ownership stake in a pool of mortgages. They can also be called a financial security or obligation for which mortgages underlie the instrument.

Such a security offers one of three different means for the investor getting paid. It might be that the loan becomes paid back utilizing principal and interest payments that come in on the pool of mortgages which back the instrument. This would make them pass through securities. A second option is that the security issuer could provide payments to the investing party independently of the incoming cash flow off of the borrowers. This would then be a non-pass through security. The third type of security is sometimes referred to as a modified-pass through security. These securities provide the security owners with a guaranteed interest payment each month. This happens whether or not the underlying incoming principal and interest payments prove to be sufficient to cover them or not.

Pass-through securities are not like non-pass through securities in key ways. The pass through ones do not stay on the issuer of the securities' or originators' balance sheets. Non-pass through securities do stay on the relevant balance sheet. With these non pass through variants, the securities are most frequently bonds. These became mortgage backed bonds. Investors in the non-pass through types often receive extra collateral as a letter of credit, guarantees, or more equity capital. This type of credit enhancement is delivered by the insurer of the mortgage backed obligation. The holder of the MBO will be able to count on the security which underlies the instruments in the event that the repayments the pools of mortgages make are not enough to cover the payments (or fail altogether) for the bond holder investors.

These offerings of Mortgage Backed Obligations, Mortgage Backed Bonds, or Mortgage Backed Securities are all ultimately backed up by mortgage pools. Analysts and investors usually call these securitized mortgage offerings. When such types of investments are instead backed up by different kinds of assets and collateral then they have another name. An example of this is the Asset Backed Securities or Asset Backed Bonds. They are backed up with such collateral as car loans, credit card receivables, or even mobile home loans. Sometimes they are referred to as Asset Backed Commercial Paper when the loans that underlie them are short term loan pools.

With these Mortgage Backed Obligations, they are often grouped together by both risk level and maturity dates. Issuers, investors, and analysts refer to this grouping as tranches, which are the risk profile-organized groups of mortgages. These complicated financial instrument tranches come with various interest rates, mortgage principle balances, dates of maturity, and possibilities of defaulting on their repayments. They are also highly sensitive to any changes in the market interest rates. Other economic scenarios can dramatically impact them as well. This is particularly true of refinance rates, rates of foreclosure, and the home selling rates.

It helps to look at a real world example to understand the complexity of Mortgage Backed Obligations and Collateralized Mortgage Obligations like these. If John buys an MBO or CMO that is comprised of literally thousands of different mortgages, then he has real potential for profit. This comes down to whether or not the various mortgage holders pay back their mortgages. If just a couple of the mortgage-paying homeowners do not pay their mortgages while the rest cover their payments as expected, then John will recover not only his principal but also interest. On the other hand, if hundreds or even thousands of mortgage holders default on their payments and then fall into foreclosure, the MBO will sustain heavy losses and will be unable to pay out the promised returns of interest and even the original principal to John.

Mortgage Backed Securities (MBS)

Mortgage backed securities turn out to be a special kind of asset which have underlying collections of mortgages or individual mortgages that back them. To be qualified as an MBS, the security also has to be qualified as rated in one of two top tier ratings. Credit ratings agencies determine these ratings levels.

These securities generally pay out set payments from time to time which are much like coupon payments. Another requirement of MBS is that the mortgages underlying them have to come from an authorized and regulated bank or financial institution.

Sometimes mortgage backed securities are called by other names. These include mortgage pass through or mortgage related securities. Interested investors buy or sell them via brokers. The investments have fairly steep minimums. These are generally $10,000. There is some variation in minimum amounts depending on which entity issues them.

Issuers are either a GSE Government Sponsored Enterprise, an agency company of the federal government, or an independent financial company. Some people believe that government sponsored enterprise MBS come with less risk. The truth is that default and credit risks are always prevalent. The government has no obligation to bail out the GSEs when they are in danger of default.

Investors who put their money into these mortgage backed securities lend their money to a business or home buyer. Using an MBS, regional banks which are smaller may confidently lend money to their clients without being concerned whether the customers can cover the loan itself. Thanks to the mortgage backed securities, banks are only serving as middlemen between investment markets and actual home buyers.

These MBS securities are a way for shareholders to obtain principal and interest payments out of mortgage pools. The payments themselves can be distinguished as different securities classes. This all depends on how risky the various underlying mortgages are rated within the MBS.

The two most frequent kinds of mortgage backed securities turn out to be collateralized mortgage obligations (CMOs) and pass throughs. Collateralized mortgage obligations are comprised of many different pools of securities. These are referred to as tranches, or pieces. Tranches receive credit ratings. It is these credit ratings which decide what rates the investors will receive. The securities within a senior secured tranche will generally feature lesser interest rates than others which comprise the non secured tranche. This is because there is little actual risk involved with senior secured tranches.

Pass throughs on the other hand are set up like a trust. These trust structures collect and then pass on the mortgage payments to the investors. The maturities with these kinds of pass throughs commonly are 30, 15, or five years. Both fixed rate mortgages and adjustable rate ones can be pooled together to make a pass through MBS.

The pass throughs average life spans may end up being less than the maturity which they state. This all depends on the amount of principal payments which the underlying mortgage holders in the pool make. If they pay larger payments than required on their monthly mortgages, then these pass through mortgages could mature faster.

Net Asset Value

The Net Asset Value refers to a mutual fund and its per share value. It is also known by its acronym NAV. Exchange traded funds, or ETFs, can also be referenced by the NAV. These values which the companies themselves compute for investors only provide a snap shot of the NAV at a particular time and date. In either security type, the fund's per share dollar value arises from the aggregate value of every security within its portfolio minus any liabilities the fund may owe. Finally this is expressed over the total number of outstanding shares in order to arrive at the shares' ultimate NAV.

Where mutual funds are concerned, the Net Asset Value is derived one time every trading day. They utilize the closing market prices for every security within the fund's holdings in order to determine this. Once this is done, the fund is able to settle all sell and buy orders which are outstanding on the shares. These prices will be set by the NAV of the mutual fund in question for the value per the trade date. Investors will always be required to wait to the next day in order to obtain their actual trade-in or trade-out price.

Because mutual funds do pay out nearly all their capital gains and income, such NAV changes are never the optimal gauge for the performance of the given fund. Instead these are better determined by looking at the yearly aggregate return, or total return.

With ETFs, these are actually closed end types of funds. This means that they actually trade more like stocks do. The shares of these Exchange Traded Funds therefore constantly trade at the market value. It might be a literal value which is higher than the NAV. This would be trading at a premium to the Net Asset Value. It could similarly trade under the NAV. This would mean the prices were trading at a discount to the NAV.

With these ETFs, the Net Asset Value becomes computed once at the markets' close so that the fund can correctly report the ETF values. During the day however, these are figured differently than the mutual fund computations. This is because the ETFs will compile the during-the-day NAV in real time at numerous points in every minute of the trading day.

It is helpful to consider an example of how the mutual funds compute their Net Asset Value calculations. The formula is actually very straightforward. It is simply that the NAV is equal to the mutual fund's assets less its liabilities with the difference divided by the total number of shares outstanding. The assets in the case of mutual funds include cash equivalents and cash, accrued income, and receivables. The main portion of their assets commonly are their investments, which will be priced per the end of the day closing values. Liabilities equate to the complete longer-term and shorter-term money owed, along with each accrued expense. Among these expenses will be utilities, salaries of the staff of the fund, and various operational costs for running such a fund.

Consider that the fictitious Diamond Stocks Mutual Fund counted $200 million in investments, figured utilizing the end of day closing prices of all their assets. Besides this, it has $14 million in cash equivalents and cash and another $8 million in receivables in total. The daily accrued income amounts to $150,000. Besides this, Diamond Stocks owes $26 million in its shorter-term liabilities and has $4 million of longer-term liabilities. The daily accrued expenses amount to $20,000. With 10 million outstanding shares, the net asset value would equate to $19.21 in the case of the Diamond Stocks Mutual Fund.

Net Present Value (NPV)

Net Present Value refers to a principal profitability measure that companies utilize in their corporate budget planning process. It helps them to analyze the possible ROI return on investment for a particular proposed or working project. Thanks to the involvement of time value and its depreciating effect on dollars, the NPV is forced to consider a discount rate and its compounding effect throughout the term of the entire project.

The actual Net Present Value in an investment or business project considers the point where revenue (or cash inflow) is equal to or greater than the total investment capital that funds the project or asset in the first place. This is particularly useful for businesses when they are comparing and contrasting a number of different projects or potential projects. It allows them to draw a valuable comparison of their comparative profitability levels to make sure that they only spend their limited resources, time, and management skills on the most valuable ventures. The higher the NPV proves to be, the more profitable it is as an investment, property, or project in the end.

Another way of thinking about the Net Present Value is as a measurement of how well an investment is meeting a targeted yield considering the upfront investment that the firm made. Using this NPV, companies can also determine precisely what adjustment they need in the initial investment in order to reach the hoped for yield. This assumes that all else remains constant.

Net Present Value can also be utilized to effectively visualize and quantify investments in real estate and other asset purchases in a simple formulaic expression. This is that the NPV is equal to the Current value minus the cost. In this iteration of the NPV, the current value of all anticipated future cash flow is discounted to today utilizing the relevant discount rate minus the cost of acquiring said cash flow. This makes NPV essentially the value of the project less the cost. When analysts or corporate accountants examine the NPV in this light, it becomes easy to understand how the value explains if the item being purchased (or project being funded) is more or less valuable than the cost of it in the first place.

Only three total categories of NPV ultimate values are possible for any property purchase or project funding. NPV could be a positive Net Present Value. This means that the buyers will pay less than the true value of the asset. The NPV might also be a Zero NPV. This simply means that the buyer or project funder is paying precisely the value of the asset or project worth. With a negative NPV in the final categorization, the buyer will be paying too much for the asset technically. This will be more than the asset is actually worth. There are cases where companies or buyers might be willing to pursue a project or acquire an asset with a negative NPV when other factors come into play.

For example, they might be interested in purchasing a property for a new corporate headquarters whose NPV is negative. The reasoning behind such a decision could be the unquantifiable and intangible value of the location of the property either for visibility purposes or because it is next to the present company headquarter premises.

It is always helpful to look at a concrete example to de-mystify difficult concepts like Net Present Value. Consider a corporation that wishes to fully analyze the anticipated profits in a project. This given project might need an upfront $10,000 investment to get it off the ground. In three years time, the project is forecast to create revenues amounting to $2,000, $8,000, and $12,000. This means that the project is expected to provide $22,000 on the initial $10,000 outlay.

It would appear that the return will amount to 120 percent for a gain greater than the initial investment. There is a reason why this is not the case though. The discount rate for the time value of money has to be factored in, and this means a percentage of several points per year at least. The figure of 4.5 percent is often utilized on a three year project like this. This takes into consideration the fact that dollars earned three years from now will not be so valuable as today's earned dollars. This is why the corporate accountants will use business calculators in order to plug in the discount time value rates to figure the true NPV. Discounting by the 4.5 percent means that the project actually will return somewhere near $21,000 in terms of today's dollar value.

Net Profit

Net Profit refers to the remaining sales dollars which are left over after a firm pays for all of its operating costs, interest on debt, preferred stock dividends, and taxes. Common stock dividends are not included in the amounts deducted from the firm's aggregate sales revenue. Sometimes analysts call this type of profit the net income, the bottom line, and/or the net earnings.

A simplistic (but useful) way of thinking about this form of profit is that it is all of the money which remains after all of the expenses of the going concern are paid in full. Calculating the net income is done when aggregate expenses are subtracted from total revenue. Because these net earnings traditionally occur on the final line in an income statement, companies often refer to it as their "bottom line."

It remains true that this Net Profit is still among the most closely watched business indicators in the world of finance. Because of this, it has a substantial part in the computations of financial statement analysis and ratio analysis. Stake holders in the corporations also scrutinize this bottom line carefully since it ultimately proves to be the way they become compensated as shareholders in the firm. When corporations are unable to realize enough profits to pay their shareholders, stock prices plunge. On the other hand, when corporations are growing and in solid financial health, the more available profits become reflected in greater stock prices.

A common mistake that many individuals make is in their understanding of what net profits actually represent. Net profit is never the metric for the total cash earnings a firm realized in a certain period. The reason for this confusing fact is that income statements also showcase a range of expenses that are not cash-based. Some of these are amortization and depreciation. In order to understand the true amount of cash which corporations actually generate, investors and analysts must carefully review the cash flow statement.

In fact any changes to net profit will be constantly and thoroughly reviewed, examined, and discussed. When firms' net profits are negative or even lower than anticipated, there are a host of issues that could be causing it. It might be that the customers' experience is negative. Sales could be decreasing for one or more reasons. Expenses at the company could be out of control or simply poorly managed and monitored. New management teams may not be performing at the anticipated or promised levels.

In the end, the Net Profit will range wildly from one firm to the next and according to which industry they represent. One industry's profits will likely be substantially different from another industry's. It is not a useful comparison to make between one corporation and another since these profits are quantified in dollars (Euros, pounds, Swiss francs, or yen). It is also a fact that no two corporations will be exactly the same size by either revenues or assets.

This is why many analysts prefer to make comparisons between corporations and industries by utilizing what they call profit margin. This is the net profit of a company as a percentage amount of its total sales. Sometimes analysts and investors will also look at the P/E Price to Earnings Ratio alternatively. This widely cherished ratio reveals to considering investors what the price is (in the form of stock price) for every dollar of net profit the corporation actually generates.

Analysts still like the metric of net profit despite these limitations. A survey conducted querying around 200 marketing managers who were senior level revealed that an incredible 91 percent agreed that they believe this measurement to be very useful.

Offshore Bonds

Offshore Bonds are sometimes called offshore investment bonds. These investment vehicles allow individuals to gain control over what point they pay tax, to whom they will pay such tax, and how much they will ultimately pay in the end. These types of bonds are offered internationally from some of the mega global multinational life insurance firms like Britain's Old Mutual International and Friends Provident International, Genarali Worldwide, RL360, and Zurich International.

Such Offshore Bonds would not ever be domiciled in the United Kingdom or the United States. Rather they would be based in such offshore tax havens as Luxembourg, Guernsey in the Channel Islands, or the Isle of Man. More and more these days, international expatriates choose Dublin, Ireland for a domicile for these investments. This is because of the perception that Ireland offers tax efficiency and effective regulatory protection.

When money like this is not brought back into most countries (beside the United States) where the citizen is from in the form of either capital appreciation or income, then it will not be subject to those jurisdictions' taxes. This is why investors have to consider the tax jurisdiction where they are residents when they cash out their Offshore Bond. It means that selecting the best location and provider of the bond is extremely critical, since this will determine which access and taxation rules apply in the event of a cash out scenario.

A great number of the Offshore Bonds prove to be inexpensive, completely transparent, and tax efficient planning investment vehicles. Investors still have to be careful that they are not abusing this type of tax and investment vehicle. Reality is that whether a bond is offshore or onshore, it truly is an investment masquerading as an insurance contract. This delivers to the investors an array of some helpful tax benefits.

There are a number of good reasons for why investors (and especially those who are not U.S. citizens who can not escape from their own taxing regime the IRS no matter where they live unless they give up their citizenship) utilize such investment vehicles as Offshore Bonds. For starters, an offshore bond will not be considered an income generating asset. Because of this truth, trustees and individuals do not have to fill in any tax returns which require self assessment.

Income which is reinvested in the Offshore Bonds will not produce income tax events. These bonds have advantages over pensions and retirement accounts as well, since investors can assign them to another individual or legal entity at will. Money kept inside of the bond may be switched around and still will not require any Capital Gains Tax payment or even tax reporting situations.

There are similarly income tax-free events with these Offshore Bonds. It is possible to draw out as much as five percent of the premium originally deposited or paid without creating any taxing liability. This can be done over a span of 20 consecutive years. When owners make their five percent withdrawals, this is not an income-generating event, but instead simply a return of original capital to the bond holder. These bonds may also be put inside of a trust and then removed from it without creating an income taxing event.

Without a doubt, these Offshore Bonds have proven to be enormously popular with expatriates living abroad. They provide tremendous possible tax advantages for anyone who will reside outside of their native country (besides for citizens of the U.S.). The reason for this is that investors are able to claim tax relief for those gains which they make when residing offshore. This significant benefit is known as time apportionment relief.

For British residents as an example, they are able to lower the tax which must be paid commiserate with the amount of time they resided outside of the United Kingdom. So if they were bondholding residents of Spain for half the life of holding the bond, then this would lower the amount of taxes they had to pay for any income or gains in Britain by half.

The danger of course is that some commission-based financial advisors will try to take advantage of the investors in this type of program. When they are not correctly established with extreme transparency, the unscrupulous financial advisor may draw out a significant amount of the savings percentage wise. This transfer of wealth is not illegal, as it is merely a case of high fees and commissions. These Offshore Bonds can be dangerously opaque if investors are not careful.

Operating Cash Flow (OCF)

Operating Cash Flow is also known by its abbreviated acronym OCF. It refers to a metric for the quantity of cash which a corporation or company's typical daily business operations produce. As such, it provides a good insight into a firm's ability to generate enough cash flow in order to either grow or at the very least maintain its existing operations. It might also prove that a going concern requires outside financing in order to fund its expansion plans.

Publically traded firms must calculate their Operating Cash Flows through employing an indirect method of calculation. This GAAP Generally Accepted Accounting Principles mandate means that they have to adjust their net income into a cash basis. They do this by making alterations to their accounts that are not cash. This includes accounts receivable, depreciation categories, and inventory changes.

In fact the Operating Cash Flow is a true representation of the cash portion of the firm's net income. This will also take into account other non-cash items thanks to the requirements which the GAAP sets out for net incomes to be done as accrual-based reporting. This means that amortization, compensation which is based upon stock shares, and incurred but as of yet not paid for expenses would be included in the calculations.

Besides this the actual net income has to be adjusted to reflect changes to working capital kinds of accounts in the balance sheet of the corporation. Especially important is the fact that any accounts receivable increases actually equate to booked revenues for which no collections have been completed. Because of this, these increases have to be taken off of the net income figure. This is partially offset at least by any reported accounts payable increases that are due but as of yet not paid, since this remains in the net income number.

Analysts have opined that such Operating Cash Flow represents the most accurate and basic form of outflows and inflows of cash as a company engages in its normal operations of the daily business. Where the health of a firm is concerned, this represents among the most crucial of metrics. Yet it most appropriately and usefully works for those corporations that are not overly complex.

The Operating Cash Flows focus on the both outflows and inflows which a corporation's principal business activities involve. This includes buying and selling inventory, paying employee salaries, and delivering services. It is important to remember that all financing and investing activities will not be included in the Operating Cash Flow. These become reportable separately. A part of these excluded activities would be purchasing equipment and factories, borrowing money, and engaging in share holder dividend payouts. Finding this cash flow number is easy by looking at the corporation's cash flows statement. This statement will break out the numbers into several categories including cash flows from operations, from financing, and from investing.

Operating Cash Flow is a very important number on a company balance sheet. Many financial analysts and investors would rather consider such cash flow measures since they reduce the impacts of confusing and opaque accounting tricks. It also delivers a better, sharper big picture for the business operations' health and reality.

Consider the following examples. When a firm concludes a big sale, this delivers a major increase to its revenues. This is irrelevant though if the firm can not collect on the money owed. It does not represent a real gain for the corporation. At the same time, firms could be producing elevated operating cash flow numbers. Despite this, they might have an abysmally low net income number if they employ an accelerated depreciation calculation or possess many fixed assets.

OTC Bulletin Board (OTCBB)

The OTC Bulletin Board (OTCBB) proves to be a service for electronic trading that the NASD National Association of Securities Dealers maintains and provides to investors and dealers. It delivers live quotes on volume and pricing data to both investors and traders on stocks which trade OTC over the counter.

Every company which is listed on this backwater exchange has to be current in its filings of financial statements with regulatory oversight group the SEC Securities and Exchange Commission or some other applicable regulatory body. Other than this, there are no minimum listing requirements on the OTC Bulletin Board exchange; unlike with sister monster exchanges the NYSE New York Stock Exchange or the NASDAQ.

The OTCBB turns out to be a fairly young stock quoting system. It began in 1990 following the passage of the Penny Stock Reform Act of 1990. This legislation mandated that the SEC had to come up with some form of system for electronic quotes for those firms which were not able to qualify for listing on one of the rival major stock exchanges such as NYSE or NASDAQ. Those securities which trade on the over the counter basis does so between individuals who are utilizing either phones or computers to place trades. Every stock which trades on the OTCBB contains an ".OB" in its suffix.

It is important for potential investors in OTC Bulletin Board stocks to remember that this is not an extension of any major stock exchange. Instead, it is because these stocks are not well known, heavily traded, or largely capitalized that they are trading on the over the counter electronic quoting system basis in the first place.

These stocks are well known for their substantial risk and rampant instability and volatility. This is why the very few of the OTCBB stocks which enjoy great success eventually migrate over to the NASDAQ or even NYSE once they are able to meet the strict listing requirements of the relevant larger exchanges. The bid-ask spreads on OTCBB are commonly much higher since the volume is so much less.

OTC Bulletin Board serves a critically important role and fills a much-needed vacuum with its existence and services. In truth there are many individual tiny companies which will never qualify for the stronger listing requirements so that their issues are allowed to trade on the major national stock exchanges.

The OTCBB gives them another avenue to float stock shares to a national investor audience so that they can obtain significant capital for their expansion needs. As long as investors recall that this is not a true exchange in any practical sense of the word, but merely an electronic quotation system, then investors will go into a potentially severely loss-making investment scenario with their eyes wide open. These securities which trade through the OTC Bulletin Board are actually a bunch of shares that exist in a tangled web of market makers who are trading them using the various quotes the system provides on a secure network computer which is only accessible by pay to play subscribers.

Another form of exchange network trading is via the so-called Pink Sheets. There are some parallels between the two systems. They are not at all related in fact though. Pink Sheets is an individually and privately held company which offers its own proprietary system of quotations. Companies whose securities trade as part of the Pink Sheets are not required to file any financials with the SEC. They also do not have to make any certain minimum docs available to members of the public or investing community at large. This is why some smaller firms prefer the simplicity and anonymity provided by the Pink Sheets operations and service.

Paper Investments

Paper investments can be several things. Where businesses are concerned, paper investments turn out to be investments in commercial paper. Commercial paper investments prove to actually be money market instruments that companies and banks sell to raise money. There are many large issuers with good credit who offer these types of paper investments to interested investors. They represent inexpensive other sources of short term funding as opposed to standard bank loans.

Commercial paper investments come with a fixed maturity of from one day to two hundred and seventy days. These types of paper investments are generally regarded as extremely secure, although they are unsecured loans. The companies that take advantage of them are commonly utilizing these short term operating funds for working capital or inventory purchases.

Corporations like to utilize commercial paper because they are able to quickly and effectively raise significant sums of money without having to get involved with costly SEC registration through selling paper investments. This can be done through working with independent dealers, or on their own efforts directly to investors. Institutional buyers commonly prove to be significant buyers of these types of paper investments.

Such notes come with amounts and maturity dates that can be specifically crafted to meet particular needs. The key features of these types of paper investments are that they are of short term maturity, commonly ranging from only three to six months of time. They liquidate on their own, with no action being required by the investing party in question. There is little to no speculation involved in their intended use as well. This gives them an appeal of clarity.

Offering this type of paper investments offers several advantages for the issuer as well. The issuer is able to access cash at rates that are lower than those offered at the bank. Companies taking advantage of commercial paper are able to leave open reserves of borrowing power at their area banks. Finally, they are capable of getting cash on hand which will allow them to benefit from trade creditors who offer special discounts for those who pay for supplies and other needs with cash.

Where traditional investments are concerned, paper investments also prove to be investments whose value is stated on and represented by paper. A number of different kinds of popular investments in the United States qualify as paper investments. These include stocks, bonds, mutual funds, certificates of deposits, and money market accounts. Shares of stock are pieces of paper that relate a certain percentage of ownership in a publicly traded company.

Most any type of investment that does not have a physical component of the investment associated with it is considered a paper investment. Commodities, as well as futures and options on futures that permit you to take delivery of the underlying commodities if you wish, represent examples of investments that are not only paper investments. These types of investments, along with real estate holdings, are considered to be physical, or hard, investments.

Passive Income

Passive income refers to money that, once it is arranged and established, does not require additional work from the person getting it. A variety of different types of passive income exist. Among them are movie, music, book, screenplay, television, and patent royalties. Other samples of passive income include click through income, rental income, and revenue from online advertising.

Activities that lead to passive income have something in common. They usually need a great amount of money, time, or both invested in them upfront to get them started. There are financial means to establishing passive income as well. You could purchase a rental property or choose to invest in a partnership or other form of company where you are a silent partner. The income that you derive from these investment activities is deemed to be passive.

Various other kinds of passive income do not need a great deal of financial investment made in them, but instead require great amounts of effort, time, and even creativity to achieve. More than a year can be required to either build up a popular website that can contribute passive income from advertising or to write a great novel. Making money from such passive income that is actually profit may take longer.

Books are a good example of how long it can take to actually make money from passive income. Publishers generally get to recover all of their printing and promoting costs, as well as any advance monies given to authors, before royalties are created and paid. Books that sell poorly could turn out to pay the author little to nothing.

Websites have a different set of challenges for their creators. There has to be more than simply good content to make money from them. They must similarly rank high in the search engine results for the necessary amount of visitors to find and go to the website. Unless a great number of visitor hits are recorded on a website, the passive income that is generated will be negligible or even none.

People are willing to put in such a huge amount of time with little assurance of results because they know that the passive income generating activity will create money for them around the clock for years to come, if it is successful. This means that passive income money is constantly being made, even when the person is asleep or on vacation. If you are able to get one passive income project up and running well, then you can attempt others. This way, you might hope to develop a few different income streams that result in a significant annual revenue which can even support you.

Many investors believe that passive income is the most superior kind that you can achieve. This is why rental properties can be so popular. Even though they can require a significant amount of maintenance work and tenant management, they can provide substantial income once several such properties are owned and made profitable.

Portfolio Income

Portfolio income proves to be money that is actually brought in from a group of investments. The portfolio commonly includes all of the various types of investments that an investor owns. These include bonds, stocks, mutual funds, and certificates of deposit. These various financial instruments earn a variety of different types of passive income, such as dividends, interest income, and capital gain distributions. Such portfolio income returns are generated by the holdings of the various investment products in the portfolio.

Portfolio income varies with the types of investments that an investor picks. You as an investor will commonly look at two different factors when assembling a portfolio for portfolio income. These turn out to be the money that the investment itself will produce, which is also known as an investment's return, and the investment's risk level that it contains.

As an example, stocks are frequently deemed to be investments with considerable risk, yet the other side of the risk return equation is that they provide income from a company's dividends, or distribution earnings returned to the shareholders, as well as an increase in the stock price as the stock value gains with time. Certificates of deposit and bonds create interest income that is paid out on the investment that you hold. Still different kinds of investments produce other types of income, although this depends on the characteristics of the investment in question.

To maximize the portfolio income while reducing the amount of risk involved, individuals commonly choose to invest in numerous different kinds of investments. This is known as diversifying your portfolio and portfolio income. This way, you can combine both safer investments that provide lower real returns with riskier investments that offer greater investment returns. Your total collection of investments is the portfolio that makes your portfolio income for you.

This portfolio income is also classified as passive income, or income that does not require you to perform any work in order to make the money. The upfront investment actually creates the income without you having to be actively involved in the money making process. This stands in contrast to incomes that are earned through active involvement, or active income that you must expend both energy and time to create.

The ultimate goal for you with your portfolio income will probably be to build up enough of it that you are capable of living off of only the income that the portfolio generates. Once this point is reached, you would be able to not receive a payroll check any longer. Instead, you would support yourself in retirement from the dividends, interest, and capital gains created by the investments in the form of portfolio income. The best and safest way to do this is to only draw on the portfolio income itself, without drawing down the original principal.

By not touching the investment principal, you allow your portfolio and resulting portfolio income to build up over time. If you do not take out the portfolio income, then the total value of the portfolio will grow faster with time, allowing you to compound your investments for retirement. It is critical to have enough money saved for retirement that you do not need to take out this principal to support yourself. Sufficient portfolio income should be generated to cover the monthly retirement expenses. In this way, you will not be reducing your principal and risking the very real danger of your portfolio running out of money while you are still alive to need it.

Purchasing Power Parity (PPP)

Purchasing power parity is a method for comparing the various standards of living of different countries and through different times. It also allows economists to compare one nation's economic productivity to another nation's. This economic theory believes that it is possible to compare the various currencies of different countries by analyzing the cost of a basket of goods. The idea states that two currencies are at a fair market value to each other when the basket of goods becomes priced identically in the two countries.

There is a formula for calculating purchasing power parity. It is $S = P1/P2$. S stands for the exchange rate of a first currency against a second one. P1 is the symbol for the price of goods in the first currency. P2 symbolizes the price of goods in the second currency.

Coming up with a meaningful comparison of goods requires that a considerable range of services and goods should be analyzed. This requires gathering a great amount of information. To help make the process easier, the United Nations worked with the University of Pennsylvania in 1968 to establish the International Comparisons Program.

The purchasing power parity numbers which come from the ICP uses price surveys from around the world which compare and contrast costs for literally hundreds of different goods. These results give international economists the tools they need to create global growth and productivity estimates.

The World Bank compiles a special report on PPP once each three years to compare the nations of the world by both U.S. dollars and their PPP values. Both the OECD Organization for Economic Cooperation and Development and the IMF International Monetary Fund base their recommended policies and economic predictions on the purchasing power parity measurements.

Forex traders have also been known to employ PPP to scout for undervalued and overvalued currencies. Finally investors with foreign corporation stocks or bonds can consider these figures to forecast how exchange rate fluctuations will impact the economy of the country where their investments are based.

When individuals or companies employ PPP, they are utilizing it in place of the market determined exchange rates. This figure provides them with the quantity of currency required to purchase the basket of goods and services used in the equation. This means that inflation rates and cost of living ultimately determine a nation's PPP.

Economists are also able to utilize purchasing power parity to determine which countries have the largest amount of purchasing power. To do this, they take the GDP gross domestic product of countries as a starting point. This is the aggregate dollar amount of every good and service a nation produces in a particular year. The number is among the preferred means of analyzing the economy of a country. Economists can determine this in either market exchange rates or PPP terms.

The PPP measurement will consider the costs of localized services and goods of a given nation as measured in U.S. prices. It contemplates both the inflation rates and the exchange rates in this calculation. The GDP using PPP demonstrates a citizen's purchasing power compared to that of the citizen in another. Since a shirt will usually cost more in one nation than in the other one, purchasing power parity helps to make the calculation fairer. While the 2016 rankings for GDP by market exchange terms show the top five countries as the U.S., China, India, Japan, and Germany, when PPP is used, China ranks ahead of the U.S.

Rate of Return

In the worlds of finance and business, the rate of return, also known by its acronym ROR, proves to be the ratio of money lost or gained pertaining to an investment and the sum of money that is originally invested in it. This rate of return is also called the rate of profit or more commonly the return on investment, or ROI.

The sum of money that is lost or gained could be called the loss or profit, interest, or even net loss or net income. Regarding the money that is actually invested, it is sometimes called the capital, asset, or principle. It is also referred to as the cost basis of an investment. Rate of return or Return on Investment is commonly stated as a percentage and not a fraction.

This rate of return is one measurement of how much cash is made or lost as a direct result of the investment in question. It quantifies the amount of income stream or cash flow that moves from the investment itself to the investor as a percentage of the original amount that the investor put into the investment. Such cash flow that accrues to the investor comes in a number of forms. It might be interest, profit, capital gains and losses, or dividends received. These capital gains and losses happen as the investment's sale price is greater or less than its initial purchase price. The use of the term cash flow includes everything except for the return of the original invested money.

Rates of return can be figured up as averages covering a number of different time periods. They may also be determined for only one time frame. When these calculations are being made, it is important not to mix up annualized and annual rates of return. Annualized rates of return prove to be geometric average returns figured up over several or even numerous periods. Annualized returns might be the investment return on a period less than or greater than a year, for example for six months or three years. The rates of return are then multiplied out or divided in order to come up with a one year rate of return that can be compared against other annual rates of return. As an example, if an investment possessed a one percent rate of return per month, then this might be more appropriately expressed as an annualized rate of return of twelve percent. Or, if you had a three year rate of return amounting to fifteen percent, then you could say that this is a five percent annualized rate of return.

Annual rates of return are instead returns figured up for single time frame periods. These time frames are commonly one year periods running from the first of January to the last day of December. Alternatively, they could cover any year long period, regardless of what month and day they started and ended.

Return on Assets (ROA)

Return on Assets is also known by its acronym ROA. It is also sometimes called return on investment. This proves to be an indicator of a company's profitability compared to its aggregate asset base. With ROA, investors and analysts can learn about the big picture of the efficiency of an organization's management compared to the deployment of their company assets which produces earnings.

This is figured up relatively easily. To calculate the ROA, simply take the corporation's annual earnings (or income) and divide these by the firm's total assets. The final answer is the percentage amount of ROA. Other investors will do a slight variation on the formula by adding back in the corporate interest costs to the net income. This allows them to employ operating returns before the net cost of debt.

Thanks to Return on Assets, analysts and investors can learn the amount of earnings that the invested capital or assets produced. Such a figure ranges dramatically from one publically traded company to the next. Every industry's ROA varies substantially. For this reason, analysts prefer to compare and contrast the ROA primarily against the company's own prior figures or alternatively versus another company which is both similar and in the same industry.

Company assets are made up of equity and debt together. The two kinds of financing will jointly fund most corporations' various operations and projects. Because of this Return on Assets number, investors are able to discern the efficiency with which the firm converts its investable money into actual net income. Higher ROA numbers are always considered to be superior. They mean that the corporations can bring in larger revenues and earnings on a smaller amount of investment.

Consider a real world example for clarification. If Imperial Legends Strategy Games produces a net income of $2 million on aggregate underlying assets of $6 million, then it has a Return on Assets of 33.3 percent. Another company Joy Beverages may enjoy the same earnings but against a full asset base of $12 million. Joy Beverages would have an ROA of only 16.7 percent in this scenario. This means that ILSG does twice the job of converting its all around investments into profits as does Joy Beverages.

This matters because it speaks volumes of the quality of management. There are not too many managers who are able to turn over significant profits utilizing small investments.

The Return on Assets provides observers with a snapshot and analysis of a business that is distinctive from the usual return on equity formula. Consider that certain industries need to pay more careful attention to the ROA figure than other ones do. In banking, some firms managed to avoid the various banking crises of the last few decades. The ones that sidestepped the problems better than others had something in common. It was that they were more conservative based on the ROA they deployed. The more successful banks did not allow their return on assets numbers to become too unnaturally high. They did this by contemplating the underlying fine details in the loan book. Too many loans that yielded too high a return indicated that management was taking excessive risks. Yet in the business of software development firms, these enterprises are not leveraged, so this ROA comparison is less important.

An important difference separates asset turnover from Return on Assets. Asset turnover specifies that companies have sales which amount to a certain amount per asset dollar on the corporate balance sheet. Conversely, the ROA explains to investors the amount of post tax profit that a firm creates for every $1 of assets it has. This is to say that the ROA compares all of the company earnings relating to the entire resource base the company claims, including both long-term debt and the capital from shareholders. This makes the relevant ROA a strict test of shareholder returns. When companies possess no debt, then their two figures of ROA and ROE Return On Equity will be identical.

Return on Equity (ROE)

Return on equity proves to be a useful measurement for investors considering a given company. This is because it takes into account three important elements of a company's management. This includes profitability, financial leverage, and asset management. Looking at the effectiveness of the management team in handling the three factors gives you as an investor a good picture of the kind of return on equity that you can expect from an investment in such a company.

Return on equity is very easy to calculate. You can figure it up by collecting two pieces of information. You will need the company earnings for a year and the value of the average share holder equity for the same year. Getting the earnings' figure is as simple as looking up the firm's Consolidated Statement of Earnings that they filed with the Securities and Exchange Commission. Alternatively, you might look up the earnings of each of the last four quarters and add them up.

Determining share holder equity is easiest by looking at the company's balance sheet. Share holder equity, which proves to be the difference of total liabilities and total assets, will be listed for you there. Share holder equity is a useful accounting construct that reveals the business assets that they have created. This share holder equity is most commonly listed under book value, or the quantity of the share holders' equities for each share. This is also an accounting book value of a corporation that is more than simply its market value.

To come up with the return on equity, you simply divide the full year's earnings by the average equity for that year. This gives you the return on equity. Companies that produce significant amounts of share holder equity turn out to be solid investments, since initial investors are paid off using the money that the business operations generate. Companies that create substantial returns as compared to the share holder equity reward their stake holders generously by building up significant amounts of assets for each dollar that is invested into the firm. Such enterprises commonly prove to be able to fund their own operations internally, which means that they do not have to issue more diluting shares of stock or take on extra debt to continue operating.

The return on equity can also be utilized to determine if a corporation is a cash generating machine or a cash consuming entity. The return on equity will simply show you this when you compare their actual earnings to the share holder equity. You can learn at almost a glance how much money the company's present assets are producing. As an example, with a twenty percent return on equity, every original dollar put into the company is creating twenty cents of real assets. This is also useful in comparing subsequent cash investments in the company, since the return on equity percentage will demonstrate to you if these extra invested dollars match up to the earlier investments for effectiveness and efficiency.

Return on Investment (ROI)

ROI is the acronym for return on investment. This return on investment is among the most often utilized methods of determining the financial results that will arise from business decisions, investments, and actions. ROI analysis is used to compare and contrast both the timing and amount of investment gains directly with the timing and amount of investment costs. Higher returns on investment signify that the results from investments are positive when you compare them against the costs of such investments.

Over the past couple of decades, this return on investment number has evolved into one of the main measurements in the decision making process of what types of assets and equipment to buy. This includes everything from factory equipment, to service vehicles, to computers. ROI is similarly utilized to determine which budget items, programs, and projects should be both approved and allocated funds. These cover every type of activity from recruiting, to training, to marketing. Finally, return on investment is often employed in choosing which financial investments are performing up to expectations, as with venture capital investments and stock investment portfolios.

Return on investment analysis is actually used for ranking investment returns against their costs. This is done by setting up a percentage or ratio number. With the vast majority of return on investment calculation methods, ROI's that are higher than zero signify that the returns on the investment are higher than the associated expenses with it. As a greater number of investments and business decisions compete for funding anymore, hard choices are increasingly made using the comparison of higher returns on investment. Many companies believe that this yields the better business decision in the end.

There is a downside to relying too heavily on the return on investment as the only consideration for making such business and investment decisions. Return on investment does not tell you anything regarding the anticipated costs and returns and if they will actually work out as forecast. Used alone, return on investment also does not explain the potential elements of risk for a given investment. All that it does is demonstrate how the investment or project returns will compare against the costs, assuming that the investment or project delivers the results that are anticipated or expected.

This limitation is not unique to return on investment, but similarly plagues other financial measurements. Because this is the case, intelligent investment and business analysis also relies on the likely results of other return on investment eventualities. Other measurements should also be used along side the return on investment to help measure the risks that accompany the project or investment.

Wise decision makers will demand more from return on investment figures than simply a number. They will require effective suggestions from the person making the return on investment analysis. Among these inputs that they will desire are the means of increasing an ROI's gains, or alternatively the means for improving the ROI through decreasing costs.

Risk Arbitrage

Risk arbitrage is also known as statistical arbitrage. It is different from pure arbitrage as it involves risk or speculation. It is also far more accessible to retail traders than real arbitrage. Because of the reasonably high probability that risk arbitrage offers traders, experts generally consider it to be playing the odds. Despite the risk involved, this form of arbitrage has grown to be among the most practiced type by retail traders. Three main types of this arbitrage exist, liquidation, merger and acquisition, and pairs trading arbitrage.

Liquidation arbitrage is a kind that involves determining the liquidation value of a business' assets. If a company possesses a book value of $100 per share and trades at $70 per share, it falls under this type. If the company determines it will liquidate, there would be an opportunity to make $30 per share on the dissolution of the company. When bigger companies practice this they buy companies whose parts are worth more than the whole of the company. They then sell off the various parts or assets to make money.

Merger and acquisition arbitrage remain the most practiced form of the strategy. The goal is to find a company that is undervalued at its current share price. If it is selected by another company as a takeover target, then it presents opportunity. The offer for this target will raise the company share price to near this level. The earlier investors get in on such a prospect, the more they are likely to profit from it.

If the merger does not go on as planned, the share prices will probably drop. Speed is the necessary factor to make this type of arbitrage work. Traders who practice this type usually receive streaming market news and trade on Level II trading. When a merger deal is announced, these traders attempt to buy in before everyone else does.

An example of this type of a deal would be a company trading at $40 which received a takeover bid for $50. The share price will rapidly rise towards $50 but not reach it until the merger actually closes. It might move to $48 per share. Those who get in on it immediately have a chance to make as much as $10 per share, or a 25% return. Others who buy in at $48 only have a $2 per share arbitrage opportunity for 4%. So long as the takeover happens as planned, both parties will make their returns. If it fails in the end for some reason, they will both likely take losses. The amount they lose depends on the price they paid and how far the stock falls back down on the failed acquisition.

Pairs trading arbitrage may be less common than the other two but it is especially useful in sideways trading markets. The idea is that investors find stock pairs which trade at a high correlation. They could be unrelated or related so long as their historical trading chart demonstrates that they trade in near tandem. Usually pairs with the greatest likelihood of success turn out to be larger stocks competing in the same industry.

The goal is to wait until one of these pairs has a price divergence in the 5% to 7% range. The variance also needs to last for some significant amount of time like two or three trading days. Investors then buy the cheaper stock long and sell the more expensive one short.

The last step is to wait for the prices to approach each other again. Once the prices are back in line, this type of arbitrage closes the trade and pockets the percentages they were apart initially. If the investor both bought the one long and sold the other short, then the gains can be twice the percentage the pair was apart.

Securities

Securities refer to financial instruments which stand for a position of ownership in a corporation which is publically traded. These would be stock shares. They could also be a creditor-like relationship to a corporation or a government entity or agency. This security would be called a bond. They might also be an option, which is the right but not obligation to acquire and own something. A security is ultimately a financial instrument that an investor or company can sell or transfer and which represents a kind of financial holding and value. The entity or corporation which provides the security to the investors is called the issuer.

There are two principal types of securities, equities and debts. Equities refer to shareholder-held ownership of a corporation. A stock is the most common example of these equities. Equity holders may receive dividends and sell their position to another party for a capital gain when the price increases to higher than they that for which they purchased it originally.

Debt securities are proof of creditor-borrower arrangements. These stand for money which a corporation or government agency borrows and which they must repay to the creditor. The debt security has terms which outline and specify the cash amount that they have borrowed, the maturity or renewal date, and the interest rate that applies. There are many forms of these debt instruments. The most common include CDs certificates of deposit, preferred stocks, corporate and government bonds, and CMOs or CDOs which are Collateralized Mortgage Obligations or Collateralized Debt Obligations.

Besides the standard forms of debt and equity types, there are also hybrid securities. They merge features of an equity and debt security together. Equity warrants are classic examples of this type of security. These are options that a company issues which provide its holders with the ability to buy stock shares in a given time frame for a pre-determined price. Convertibles are bonds which may be transferred into stock shares of common stock in the company which issues them. Preferred shares are actual shares of stock that pay dividends or interest ahead of the common stock class of shares.

Two main organizations regulate the issuance and sale of such a security within the United States. These are the SEC Securities and Exchange Commission and the FINRA Financial Industry Regulatory Authority.

Issuers of a security like this could be one of several different types of organizations. Municipal governments can issue bonds in order to raise specific project funding. Buyers of a security might be retail investors who purchase and sell them for their own accounts. Wholesale investors are those which trade the security as a financial institution working at the instruction for their customers and clients. There are also institutional investors which are a major category of security buyers. These include insurance companies, managed funds, pension funds, and investment banks like Goldman Sachs.

The purpose of a security is to float a debt or ownership instrument so that a commercial enterprise or government agency can raise fresh capital. By selling such a security, corporations are able to create money for business purposes and acquisitions. Sometimes the demand in the market place is strong enough and the pricing arrangements are favorable enough that it makes more sense for companies to issue securities to raise money rather than choose to borrow them in the form of loans or bonds. Government entities can not issue and float stock. Instead they may only issue debt in the form of general obligation or specific revenue bonds.

Securities which companies issue in the primary market they do in the form of an IPO initial public offering. Once these shares are floated and sold, all issued shares of stock are called secondary offerings. This is the case even when they still sell them in the primary market. Companies can also privately place such securities. There are cases where both private placement and public primary market floating takes place. The secondary market is the place where such a security becomes transferred from one investor to a different investor.

Self Directed IRA

Self directed IRAs prove to be special kinds of individual retirement accounts. They are different from traditional IRAs because they provide the account holder with a significantly greater variety of investment choices and control over decisions on the account. With these types of IRAs, the owner or an investment advisor makes a variety of investment decisions. They then deliver these instructions to an IRA custodian who executes them.

Federal law allows these types of IRAs to invest in a tremendous range of investment vehicles. It is IRS section 408 that restricts the few categories that are not allowed. The IRS forbids investments of IRA funds in life insurance and collectibles such as rugs, art, gems, etc. It does allow a wide range of investment choices that cover most anything else.

Self directed IRAs may purchase real estate, mortgages and trust deeds, energy investments, gold and other precious metals in bullion form, privately held stock, privately owned LLCs and Limited Partnerships, and corporate debt or promissory notes. When accounts such as these are opened primarily to purchase precious metals bullion, they are typically known by the name of their primary metal in which they invest.

These Precious Metals IRAs can be called Gold IRAs, Silver IRAs, Platinum IRAs, and Palladium IRAs. Such self directed IRAs can even purchase franchises such as Subway or Timothy Horton. All of these different investment choices allow for superior and broad based asset diversification of investors' retirement funds.

These types of IRAs also provide all of the usual benefits which are commonly associated with Traditional IRAs. Money saved in these plans is contributed on a tax free or tax deferred basis. No taxes will be paid on either the money deposited, or the gains made on these investments within the account, until they are withdrawn at retirement or under early withdrawal rules and limitations. Self directed IRAs are still subject to the same yearly maximum contribution limits of $5,500 in 2016. They allow for larger contributions of $6,500 to be made as catch up once the account holders reach age 50.

Early withdrawals from these IRAs as with traditional ones are penalized. It is often more advantageous to take a loan against the value of the IRA rather than suffer the financial consequences of early withdrawal. When loans are taken, there is no penalty. A repayment plan is established to put the borrowed funds back in the account in installments. Loans can be approved for a variety of expenses, such as home purchase, educational needs, or health care related expenses.

When an actual early withdrawal is taken, two penalties are assessed. First the money in the account is taxed as ordinarily earned income. Next a 10% penalty is levied by the IRS on all monies which the owner early withdraws.

These types of IRAs do have some limitations. The custodian must physically hold all assets in the account. This means that the account owners are not allowed to keep their real estate or mortgage deeds, stock certificates, or precious metals bullion at home in a safe. There have been offers made by some companies to help investors become their own IRA custodian by forming a special LLC company. This is a gray area which the IRS has not yet come down on with a hard ruling. In the future, they are likely to rule that investors absolutely can not be a custodian for their own gold, silver, platinum, or palladium bullion using either a safe deposit box or a home based safe.

The IRS requires that owners of these accounts begin taking distributions no later than at age 70. They can start withdrawing them as retirement funds at 59 ½ if they wish to begin using the money earlier.

SEP IRA

SEP IRAs are special simplified employee pensions that permit employers to contribute money to the retirement plans of their employees. If individuals are self employed, they may also set up and fund one of these accounts for their own benefit. These plans compare favorably to the more popular and utilized 401(k) plan. SEPs offer greater contribution amount limits. They are also much less complicated to establish and maintain than are the 401(k)s.

Any type of employer is allowed to create an SEP IRA. This means that businesses which are not incorporated, partnerships, and sole proprietorships can all work with and utilize them. Even self employed individuals who are employed elsewhere as well (with retirement plans at their other workplace) can make their own SEP.

SEP IRAs offer several advantages to owners and contributors. They provide significant tax benefits for employees and employers. Employer contributions give tax deductions to the employer during the tax year in which they make the contribution. Self employed individuals also can take this tax deduction for themselves. SEPs are also popular because they do not require any annual paperwork to be filed with the IRS. The paperwork that creates these accounts also offers the plus of being simple and minimal.

Individuals can make contributions for SEP IRAs in the year after the contribution applies. Deadlines for these contributions may also be stretched to the tax return due date. As far as establishing these accounts goes, deadlines are for the tax return due date and any extension that the IRS grants on the taxes.

In general, these accounts have to be opened and all contributions should be made by the April 15th that comes after the year in which the income was attained. Any taxpayers who take an extension on their tax returns to October 15th would receive a similar grace period for opening and funding the SEP IRA.

The contribution amounts for SEPs are quite flexible. No set percentage has to be contributed as with some of the rival retirement accounts like Keoghs. One could contribute nothing or as much as 25% of his or her income for the year (on as high as a $265,000 income amount). The full contribution for a single individual is not allowed to be greater than $53,000 in the year 2016. This amount contrasts with the typical standard IRA contribution limits of $5,500 for the year 2016.

The SEP limits are also substantially higher than the contribution limits on 401(k)s that come in at $18,000 for 2016 or at $24,000 for those who are at least 50 years old. SEPs do not have any provisions for catch up, as with other forms of IRAs or 401(k)s. Thanks to the higher contribution limits for every given year, this does not usually present a problem for those who are behind on their retirement accounts and want to put in more.

Employers are required to treat all employee contributions equally. This means that they must give the same contribution percentage for each employee who has made at least $600 in the year, who is 21 years or older, and who has worked for the company minimally three out of five prior years.

The only point where contributions to SEP IRAs get complicated centers on maximum contribution amounts. The 25% of income limit mentioned earlier is not figured out of gross revenue, but from net profits. Besides this, deductions on the half of self employment tax have to be first taken off of the net profit number before the limit for maximum contributions can be accurately determined off of the net profits.

Simple IRA

Among the stable of various types of IRAs American savers for retirement can take advantage of is a less common plan called the SIMPLE IRA. These kinds are a combination of traditional IRAs and employer offered plans like 401(k)s. The word SIMPLE in this case is actually an acronym that stands for Savings Incentive Match Plan for Employees. This is the most common name for the employer offered tax deferred retirement savings account.

SIMPLE IRAs were created to help smaller employers who have 100 or less employees. The idea was for them to offer their workers retirement plans. The IRS knew that the bigger packages of benefits all too often involved long and difficult opening procedures with mountains of complicated paperwork. Smaller employers simply did not have the time or resource capacity to complete and maintain these types of plans.

Among the advantages of SIMPLE IRAs is that they are not governed by ERISA, the Employee Retirement Income Security Act. This means that they are able to sidestep substantial expenses and significant amounts of paperwork in establishing them. The contributions to these kinds of IRA accounts are also fairly straightforward. Employers must make specific minimum amount contributions to the accounts of the employees.

They can accomplish this by establishing a match program at a minimum of 3% of their employee contributions. Alternatively they might set a 2% of his or her salary flat rate and offer it to every employee who participates.

When employees become part of a company SIMPLE plan, they are basically establishing a traditional IRA via their employing company. A significant disadvantage to these types of IRAs centers on their lower contribution limits. These are less than comparable 401(k) plans or other plans which employers sponsor. The limits amount to $12,500 for a single year in tax years 2015 and 2016.

Rolling over from these types of IRAs is also more complicated. They can not be started without a waiting period first being observed. Once employees start their participation with the plans, they can not do a rollover for generally two years on from their participation dates. The only exception to this rule pertains to transfers between SIMPLE IRAs.

These can be done at any time since they are considered to be a tax free transfer from one trustee to another. In the even of any other type of transfer within the two years waiting period, these are deemed as distributions by the IRS. While most penalties for tax deferred plans are set at 10% withdrawal penalties, these particular IRAs carry a more punishing 25% withdrawal tax penalty.

After the conclusion of the two year time frame, individuals may then move their funds from the SIMPLE plan to a different kind of IRA. The only restriction is that they can not move them to a Roth IRA which is funded with pre-taxed dollars. The current SIMPLE plan as well as the new plan must also allow for the transfer to occur.

As with any kind of retirement plan, early withdrawal penalties apply. If any withdrawals occur before the official retirement age of 59 ½ is attained, the early withdrawal penalties of up to 25% will be assessed against the account withdrawals.

When rollovers are done, direct rollovers are much preferred to indirect rollovers. If account holders pursue indirect rollovers there are tax withholding requirements. It is also possible that the account owner will inadvertently fail to complete the transfer in time or at all and then suffer from the substantial early withdrawal tax penalties of up to 25%.

Solo 401(k) Plan

Solo 401(k) plans function much as their standard 401(k) plan cousins do, but display some important differences. These retirement savings plan vehicles for the self employed are also called One Participant 401(k)s, Self Employed 401(k)s, Individual 401(k)s, and Uni-Ks.

These particular 401(k)s provide business owners and spouses who do not have any employees beyond themselves with the ability to be a part of a 401(k) type of tax deferred plan. The plans are fairly new. Congress unveiled them as part of their 2001 Economic Growth and Tax Relief Reconciliation Act. At the time, these became the first specially tailored employer sponsored retirement plans intended for the self employed. Before their introduction, these self employed persons could only rely on such plans as IRAs, Keogh Plans, or Profit Sharing Plans.

These Solo 401(k)s possess practically identical requirements and rules as do the normal 401(k) plans. There are two important exceptions to this. The owner and the business do not find themselves governed by the expensive and complicated requirements of the ERISA Employee Retirement Income Security Act. Besides this, the company is not permitted to employ additional employees who are full time workers contributing 1,000 hours or more each year to the business.

Contributions also have their own particular rules with these Solo plans. The account owner is also both the employee and employer. For the 2016 tax year, employee contributions are limited to $18,000 (or $24,000 per year in the case of those who are fifty years of age or older). Other contributions can be put in as employer contributions. Whichever type a business owning participant wants to call these contributions, the limit for both employee and employer contributions may not be more than $53,000 for a given year.

One benefit that holders of these Solo 401(k) plans enjoy is that they do not have to employ a custodian as with IRAs. Instead they can work with practically any financial institution or bank as their account trustee. Assuming that the trustee will handle it, these plans are able to invest in a wide range of alternative asset types. This includes mutual funds, individual bonds and stocks, ETFs, CDs, real estate, life insurance, S corporations, and precious metals bullion such as gold or silver. Solo Plans are almost unique in their ability to invest in life insurance, which even the self directed IRA plans are not enabled to do.

This all makes the Solo 401(k)s practically unrivalled in their capability to provide retirement plans with low costs, that are easy to make transactions in, with great flexibility, and with generous contribution limits all at once. The downsides to the Solo 401(k) are two. Most workers are not allowed to participate with them. They also need a great deal of paperwork and account maintenance when measured up against numerous other types of retirement plans.

Rollovers are easy to do with these Solo plans. They are able to receive such transfers from other kinds of accounts and IRAs. Account holders may also transfer or roll them over to another kind of retirement account. It is important to check with the rules of an individual's particular plan, as some plans do not accept rollovers from the Solo 401(k)s. Besides this, there are Solo 401(k)s that specifically do not permit rollovers.

Business owners should take care when setting up these types of accounts. Rolling over these types of retirement vehicles will not incur any IRS tax penalties, so long as they are done according to the IRS rules and regulations. An individual has 60 days to finish the procedure and may only engage in it one time per year. Failing to abide by these rules will incur regular income taxes plus the 10% penalty for early withdrawals, unless the individual is older than the 59 ½ years retirement age.

Traditional IRA

The Traditional IRA is the most common type of the various individual retirement accounts available to savers for retirement. Besides this type of IRA, there are also SEP IRAs, Roth IRAs, and Self Directed IRAs. Each of these types of accounts has at least a few features in common with the original and still most popular plain IRA.

These accounts are all particularly designed to help save, grow, and fund individuals' retirements. They all permit investors to trade a variety of securities, such as stocks, mutual funds, ETFs, and bonds. Different from other kinds of brokerage and investment accounts, IRAs most importantly offer account holders tax benefits. The main difference between traditional IRAs and Roth IRAs centers on the way taxes are paid or deferred by the IRS rules.

With a Roth IRA, owners pay taxes on contributions now. All gains that account holders make in the account then accrue tax free for the entire life of the retirement savings vehicle. The traditional forms of IRAs give holders the advantage of tax deferred contributions. This means that they will not have to pay any taxes on money contributed until they withdraw them later on at retirement time. All gains that they earn in the account over the life of the IRA will be taxable at the time they withdraw them.

With all of these types of IRAs, the annual contribution limits remain the same. For tax year 2016, this amount is $5,500 for individual contributions or $11,000 for married individuals filing jointly. Catch up contributions are also the same in these various kinds of IRAs. When people reach age 50, they can make additional contributions amounting to $1,000 each year for an individual or $2,000 for married people filing jointly.

This means that instead of adding $5,500 individually to the IRA for the year, an individual could contribute $6,500 per year once he or she turns 50. Similarly married individuals would be allowed to add $13,000 per year instead of $11,000 annually once they both reach age 50.

Traditional IRAs do not feature any income limits while Roth IRAs do have these. People can be disqualified from making investments in their Roth IRAs if they earn too much money any given tax year. Single filers are only allowed to make less than $110,000 each year. Above this income, the contribution amount which the IRS allows tapers down until the income reaches $125,000.

Once this income limit is reached, a Roth IRA contribution is disallowed for the tax year. With married filing jointly, the income maximum is higher. With under $173,000 earned for the year, the full $13,000 maximum contribution is permitted. This amount tapers off as the earnings rise to $183,000. Beyond these earnings, two individuals who are married are not allowed to utilize the Roth IRA in that particular tax year.

IRAs are different from 401(k)s, the other popular retirement savings vehicle, in several critical ways. Traditional and the other forms of IRAs can only be set up and maintained by an individual acting on his or her own behalf. 401(k)s are retirement accounts that employers set up on behalf of their employees. Many employers make partially matching contributions to their employees' 401(k) accounts.

IRAs also commonly offer superior choices in different investment possibilities than do the more limited 401(k) plans. Self directed IRAs are allowed to invest in most any type of investment that is not considered to be a collectible item. This means that Self Directed IRAs are allowed to invest in franchises, real estate, precious metals, mortgages, energy, and other alternative investment ideas.

Trust Account

A trust account refers to a type of account which a trustee holds on the behalf of the beneficiary. The trustee does not have the ability to utilize the funds in any personal capacity, but merely to safe keep, disburse, and invest them for the advantage of the beneficiary.

An example of this type of arrangement is when an attorney holds funds for the benefit of the client. The attorney will not be able to draw upon the funds until after a certain protocol takes place. As the attorney earns the lawyer fees, the client will have to first review and then actually approve the bill from the attorney before he or she can transfer the client funds from this trust account over to the general account of the attorney for settlement of bills.

There are a number of reasons and situations in which individuals may opt to establish a trust account. In some scenarios, people wish to disperse a pre-determined sum of money to their family or other loved ones over a number of years or throughout the remainder of their natural lives.

As a real world example, consider the following. Parents may wish to establish some trust accounts which will provide money to their dependents and/or children every month if and when they die. In such a scenario, it would normally be banking brokers who would manage such accounts. In fact these broker trustees would draw down the account values by the appropriate amount every month or year as they disbursed the either monthly or yearly funds to the beneficiaries for the individuals who originally formed the trust.

There are other common kinds of trusts as well. One of these is a property tax trust account. Such accounts will be established by entrepreneurs of real estate who own a variety of properties. Rather than have to be concerned about the property tax funds and disbursements to the appropriate taxing authorities themselves, they elect to form a trust account which will pay the taxes. This prevents the entrepreneurs from forfeiting their valuable properties because they forgot to pay the property taxes. There are a number of monetary benefits to having such an account. One of these is that estate taxes will not apply to properties contained in such a trust when the owner dies.

There are two different main types of trust accounts. These are revocable and irrevocable trusts. With revocable trusts, these represent deposit accounts whose owners chose to name one or several beneficiaries. These beneficiaries would then obtain the deposits in the account once the holder of the account died. As the name implies, such revocable trusts may be terminated, revoked, or altered on demand whenever the holder of said account wishes. In this particular case, the owner is the trustor, settlor, or grantor of the revocable trust in question. These types of trusts will be established as either informal or formal. While trustees are powerful and have a broad scope of authority over the assets of the beneficiary, they are not omnipotent, but must be bound by the laws and regulations of the jurisdiction which pertain to trust accounts.

Irrevocable trusts on the other hand are similarly deposit accounts but they are not titled in the name of the owner. Instead these become titled as an irrevocable trust for the name. The owner, trustor, settlor, or grantor also makes deposits of money or other valuable assets to the trust account. The principal difference is that the owners forfeit all ability to alter or cancel the trust once they have established it. These types of trusts also become created once an owner of a revocable type of trust dies. They can be set up through a judicial order as well, or even by a statute as appropriate.

Trust Fund

A trust fund proves to be a specific kind of legal entity. It contains property or cash which it holds to benefit another group, individual, or organization. Numerous different kinds of trusts exist. They are governed by almost as many provisions that determine how they work. Every trust fund involves three critical parties. These are the grantor, the beneficiary, and the trustee.

A grantor is the individual responsible for creating the trust fund. Grantors can do this with a variety of assets. They might give stocks, bonds, cash, mutual funds, real estate, private businesses, art, or other items of value to the fund. They also determine the terms by which the trustee will manage the fund.

Beneficiaries are the individuals who receive the benefit of the fund. The grantor sets it up on their behalf. The assets the grantor places inside of the trust fund are not the property of the beneficiary. The trustee oversees them so that the financial gain benefits this individual according to the rules laid out by the grantor at the time he or she establishes it.

Trustees are the managers of these funds. They could be an institution like a the trust department of a bank, an individual, or a number of trusted advisors. Their job is to make sure that the fund fulfills its duties spelled out by the governing law in the trust documents. Trustees typically receive small management fees. The trustee could manage the assets directly if the trust specifies this. In other cases, trustees have to pick out investment advisors who are qualified to manage money.

Trust funds come to life under the rules of the state legislature where the trust originates. Different states offer advantages to certain types of trusts. This depends on what the grantor wants to do by establishing the fund. This is why attorneys help to draft the trust documents to make sure they are correct and most advantageous. As an example, there are states which allow perpetual trusts that can continue forever. Other states make these illegal because they do now want to enfranchise a class of future generations who receive substantial wealth for which they did not work.

Special clauses may be inserted into these trusts. Among the most heavily used is the spendthrift provision. This keeps the beneficiary from accessing the fund assets to pay debts. It also allows parents to ensure that any irresponsible children they have do not find themselves destitute or homeless despite poor decisions they may make.

Trust funds provide a large number of benefits. They receive special protection from creditors. They ensure that family members follow wills after the grantor passes away. These trusts also help estates to avoid as many estate taxes as possible so that wealth can reach a greater number of generations.

Trusts can be an ideal way to ensure the continuity of a business. Sometimes business owners wish to protect a company and their employees after they die. They might still wish for the profits to benefit their heirs. In this case, the trustee would oversee the management of the business while the heirs reaped the financial rewards but could not break up or ruin the company through mismanagement.

Trusts can also be used with life insurance to transfer significant amounts of money which will benefit the heirs. A small trust could purchase a grantor life insurance. When the grantor dies, the insurance money funds the trust. The trustee will then buy investments and give the rents, interest, and dividends to the beneficiaries.

Underlying Assets

Underlying assets refer to any asset or valuable commodity which determines the value of a derivative based upon the asset. This term is frequently and importantly utilized to discuss derivatives trading. Options are a good example of this. Derivatives themselves prove to be financial instruments that investors trade. Their price is derived from the asset that underlies them. This underlying asset will be the investible instrument like an individual stock, a stock market index, a currency or currency pair, a commodity, or futures. The price of the derivatives will be based upon these.

Options for a given stock provides the holder of the option with the right (but not the obligation) to purchase or sell the stock at a certain strike price (a given price point) on a particular date at some expiration point (a future date that is predetermined). In the case of an option, the underlying assets will always amount to the stock of the company in question.

This underlying asset helps to identify the financial instrument in the agreement that gives the contract its value. Investors in such a contract will always have the right, or option, to purchase the underlying assets for a pre-arranged price on the expiration date. The asset that underlies the contract provides the security of the agreement itself. The two trading parties consent to exchange the underlying asset if necessary as a contract clause in the derivative agreement.

Famed and legendary investor Warren Buffet has notoriously and correctly declared such derivatives to be "financial weapons of mass destruction." This proved to be the case in the Global Financial Crisis of 2008-2009. A wide range of derivatives based on shaky underlying assets literally blew up the world economy and banking system in financial carnage that is still reverberating throughout the economies of the world nearly ten years later.

Take some real world examples that will help to clarify the complex ideas. Berkshire Hathaway sells stock market index put options on worldwide stock market indices that range from the FTSE 100 in London to the American-based S&P 500. These options are unusual because the do not have an expiration date until the years ranging from January of 2018 to January of 2026. On those particular dates of the varying contracts, it will be the underlying assets of the relevant stock market indices which will decide the amount of money that Berkshire pays out to the option holders.

In theory, the indices could approach zero, though this is highly unlikely. Yet Berkshire Hathaway would be forced to come out of pocket to the amount of up to $27.6 billion to these put holders if they did. When Berkshire sold these puts, they received $4.2 billion as premiums for their risk when they sold these during the years from 2004 to 2008. Guarantor of the options and Berkshire Hathaway founder Warren Buffet has cheerfully invested these billions in premiums and made considerable returns on them since those years in which they sold them.

Another classic example surrounds PepsiCo. The California-based company always reports its earnings in U.S. dollars. Yet it has operations all over the world because of its diversified soft drinks, bottled water, chips and snacks, alternative energy drinks like PowerAde, and juices divisions. This means that it must borrow, invest, and earn money in a range of currencies on every continent. The company has utilized currency swap agreements to help reduce the volatility of changing currency exchange rates on its costs to borrow and earn money in other currencies. The underlying assets would be Euros, British pounds sterling, Canadian dollars, Australian dollars, Japanese yen, Swiss francs, and other major world currencies.

In the end, there are literally trillions worth of derivatives which derive their actual value from an underlying asset of one type or another. This might be interest rates determined in London (the now-infamous LIBOR), stock market index values, or oil and gold hard commodities. Such derivatives make it possible for investors to engage with another party in a zero sum game where the stakes depend on the rises and fails of most any asset or market in the world. Neither party has to be directly involved in the underlying market or asset, thanks to these financial weapons of mass destruction called derivatives.

US Trust

U.S. Trust today is the Bank of America Private Wealth Management division. It existed as an independent U.S. Trust Corporation from 1853 through 2000. At this time Charles Schwab and Co. acquired the bank and trust. They later sold it to Bank of America back in 2007. U.S. Trust today provides (as it has for two centuries) its clients with wealth structuring, investment management, and lending and credit facilities.

U.S. Trust has its headquarters in New York City on 114 West 47th Street in the United States. The firm counts more than 100 branch offices throughout the country across 31 different states plus Washington, D.C. They work to provide their ultra high net worth clients with specially tailored solutions and resources that help meet their needs for credit and banking, investment management, and wealth structuring. Teams of advisors serve the clientele through a wide variety of financial services. Chief among these offerings are financial and succession planning, investment management, specialty asset management, philanthropic asset management, customized credit products, family office services, family trust stewardship, and financial administration.

U.S. Trust arose in 1853 as a State of New York chartered bank. This makes it the original and also oldest such trust company within the United States. The new venture had the backing of a combination of wealthy investors who poured a million dollars into the firm which was called United States Trust Company of New York at that point.

Among the first board of trustees were thirty different influential and important New Yorkers. This included founding investor New York City Mayor Joseph Lawrence from the Bank of the State of New York who became bank trust president. Secretary of the trust went to United States Life Insurance Company of New York's John Aikman. Among the other important founders were industrialist, inventor, and philanthropist Peter Cooper; Marshall Field the department store founder; President Shepherd Knapp of Mechanics National Bank of the City of New York; and steel and iron manufacturer and railroad developer Erastus Coming.

The company became founded to serve clients of individuals and institutions as a trustee and executor of their money. This proved to be an innovative concept as trusts had not been fully conceived of at this point. It only took till 1886 for the firm to be well-established as a stable and highly regarded financial institution.

Thanks to this growing reputation, by the middle of the 1800's, the company had acquired a roster of super rich clients. It served a significant role in a number of nationally and internationally important construction projects like the Panama Canal and national American railroads. A great number of the firm's corporate clients floated securities to help finance such building project initiatives. The trust got to play the part of corporate trustee in the projects. Such a boom in enterprising and industrial projects aided the business in expanding into the management of personal trusts for the super rich as well. By the 1880's and 1890's, the firm counted such prestigious and ultra high net worth individual as William Waldorf Astor, Oliver Harriman, and Jay Gould.

The company successfully managed to survive and thrive despite a range of damaging financial crises in the last half of the 1800s and the early 1900s. In 1928, it counted over a billion dollars in trust assets. It stood well above its vastly smaller rivals. Thanks to the company's emphasis on stability, it managed to ride out the 1929 stock market crash and resulting decade long depression.

The company thrived by introducing additional specially tailored personal services in the next few decades. Among these were advising its ultra wealthy clients and families on careers, private schools, and universities for their kids. By 1958, U.S. Trust had begun its earliest ads in the newspaper society pages of The New Yorker. It was also advertising in the Metropolitan Opera and New York Philharmonic Society programs at this time.

Despite restructuring in the 1970s, 1980s, and 1990s, the company still became a takeover target by Charles Schwab and Co. in the year 2000. It ceased to be an independent prestigious outfit of nearly 150 years long at this point.

Value Investing

Value investing is the strategy that Benjamin Graham developed for investing in stocks. Warren Buffet later made it famous after he left Graham's company and went on to found Berkshire Hathaway. Buying stocks this way involved a level of discipline practiced by insurance underwriters. The method focuses on several key ideas. Investors have to consider risks involved carefully, avoid stocks which show a high amount of uncertainty, and allow a margin of safety.

Graham developed his different investing techniques while managing money as President of his Graham-Newman Corporation. He focused on net working capital investments, arbitrage, diversification, and tangible assets. Investors continue to use all of these but the first one over seventy years later.

Net working capital originally functioned as a cornerstone of value investing until changes in transparency rules and market technology made it obsolete. Net working capital investments were those where the stock's shares traded at a large 30% or higher discount to their amount of working capital.

The idea was that a value investor could buy dollar investments for effectively 70 cents or less. Some of these companies failed. This was mitigated by diversifying into many different stocks. On a combined basis, these companies brought Graham and his investors good returns. Warren Buffet utilized this category of investments heavily in his early years running the Buffet Partnership that eventually became Berkshire Hathaway.

Arbitrage proved to be the value investors' secret weapon. Graham passionately believed arbitrage would routinely provide 20% annual returns. This boosted the total return on the overall value investing portfolio. Arbitrage seeks to make money on discrepancies in price with little or even no risk.

If a company makes an offer for a rival at $60 per share, but the shares trade at $57, there is a $3 price discrepancy between that point and when the deal closes. This amounts to possibly 5% that investors can acquire in a matter of a few months. Assuming the deal closes, there is no risk in this trade. Value investors simply use arbitrage as a way to profit from a security and the money time value that is literally undervalued.

Diversification remains a critical component of Graham's investing strategy. He believed in diversifying into as many individual investments as made sense. He also practiced diversification into different kinds of asset classes. Value investing puts a certain percentage into common stocks, preferred stocks, mutual funds (which did not yet exist when Graham created the strategy), and bonds. This went along with the main premise that first investors must avoid losing their money. Receiving a good return on investment money is secondary to this idea.

Tangible assets is another value investing principle that still holds today. Graham was interested in the actual physical assets that lay behind his common or preferred stocks and bonds. This might include factories, office buildings, equipment, real estate, or rail cars. He would only buy into companies whose assets were great enough to fully back up the principle and dividend or interest payments. They would have to liquidate these assets to get back their investment money. Graham told those who valued invested to constantly look at the bonds they held and be prepared to change to other bonds if they had stronger assets.

Benjamin Graham and value investing also proved to be among the earliest groups to practice tactical asset allocation. If investors studied and determined stocks were overvalued, they should sell stocks and move money into bonds. When stocks were undervalued, he counseled investors to sell bonds and go heavier into stocks. This is still a cornerstone idea of investing today.

Venture Capital

Venture capital refers to the process of investors purchasing a portion of a start up company. Firms or individuals that engage in this are called venture capitalists. They pour money into a firm that offers a high rate of growth but that also contains high risk. The typical venture capital investment time frame generally proves to be from five years up to seven years. Such investors anticipate getting a profit back on their investment through one of two ways. Either they hope to sell their stake in an Initial Public Offering to the public, or they hope to sell the company outright.

Investors who involve themselves in venture capital investments often wish to obtain a certain percentage of the company's ownership. They might also request being given one of the director's seats. This makes it easier for the investors to ask to be given their funds back either through insisting that the company be sold or reworking the deal that they made in the first place.

Venture capitalist investments are comprised of three different kinds. One of them is early stage financing that might be broken down into seed financing, first stage financing, or start up financing. Seed financing means that a tiny dollar amount of venture capital is paid to an inventor or other entrepreneur who wants to open a business. This might be employed to come up with a business plan, do market research, or bring on a good management team.

First stage financing is the type needed as companies look to boost their capital so that they can begin full scale operations. Start up financing instead is venture capital distributed to a business that exists for under a year. In this stage, a product will not be on the market already, or will only just have been put on the market for sale.

A second type of venture capital investments is known as expansion financing. Expansion financing is comprised of both bridge financing as well as second and third stage financing. Bridge financing refers to investments that only receive interest and are short term. They are mostly employed for company restructurings. They might also be utilized to cash out early investors.

Second stage financing proves to be investment money for the purpose of growing a company already up and running. While such a company may not yet demonstrate actual profits, it is producing and selling merchandise. It also possesses inventories and accounts that are expanding.

Third stage financing is investments that venture capitalists make in companies that have at least broken even on costs or are even starting to demonstrate profits. In this case, venture capital is employed to grow the business further. For example, third stage financing could be utilized to develop more or better products, or to purchase needed real estate.

Still a different popular version of venture capital investing is known as acquisition financing. In this type of venture capital, the investment goes into gaining a stake in or the entire ownership of a different company. Management could also choose to use this venture capital to buy out yet another business or product line, whatever its development stage proves to be. They might acquire either a public or a private company in this way.